The Mindful Way
To Study

The Mindful Way
To Study

Dancing With Your Books

Jake J. Gibbs
Roddy O. Gibbs

O'CONNOR PRESS
The Mindful Way To Study: *Dancing With Your Books*
Jake J. Gibbs and Roddy O. Gibbs

Copyeditor: Ian O'Reily
Cover Design: Raden Bagus
Interior Design: Jimmy Sevilleno

Published in the United States by O'Connor Press

ISBN 978-0-9895314-1-2

In loving memory of Mary Ellen "Fuzzy" Hanrahan:
An exquisite tomato with a fine set of gams.

Table of Contents

Introduction

Read Me! Please

Hello Kind Reader,

Many of you will find the messages contained between the covers of this book to challenge much of what you've learned about learning. The purpose of our book is to help you develop a more effective approach to learning by changing the way you see it. Here are some points to consider and the central messages of the book.

The Mindful Way To Study: Dancing With Your Books

Taking the Pain Out of Studying: The study sessions and school projects you take on don't have to be an experience in misery. In the right state of mind and with the right strategies, learning and schoolwork can bring satisfaction (or at least a lot less suffering).

Change in Attitude: The mindful approach to studying is simply a change in attitude toward what you are doing. It's easy to understand, but it's not easy.

Fighting With Your Books (FWB): Many students see courses as a fight with their books. Common images include phrases like "hit the books," "conquer material," "smoke it," "nail it," "own it," "kick butt," "grind," "cram," and "ground and pound." These students are in conflict with the material and come to see their books as adversaries. *Winning* is everything. Their objective in battle is to subdue, crush, and/or dominate their books. Their mission when studying is to triumph over the material they have been assigned to learn.

Dancing With Your Books (DWB): Getting something from your books does not require vein-popping effort to give them a good thrashing. It's not a blood sport. Dancing With Your Books (DWB) is a far better approach than Fighting With Your Books (FWB). In DWB, you and your books are cooperatively engaged in a mutual enterprise. Two become one in the dance of learning.

To Get to Your Goal, Focus on Means: The mindful approach is the most effective strategy for achieving your goals (grades, degrees, job offers, and so on). The method is to set your goals, and then to allow your attention to settle on the means to reach your goals (studying, listening in class, and reading assignments, for example). It is an approach that helps you to pay full attention to what you're doing in the present to reach your objective, which is always in the future. In other words, the best way to get what you want is to direct all your attention to what you are doing to get it. The essence of the mindful way is that to get from A to B, let your mind focus on A.

Inefficiency in the Distribution of Attention: If you place all of your attention on *goals*, there isn't any left for *means* (or the work to be done to reach the goals). Even if you split your attention between what you want and how to get it, only half your effort is on the steps you have to take to reach your goals.

Mindfulness: Mindfulness is simply a way to pay attention so that you are fully in the present moment. It entails gently allowing your mind to return to what you are doing when you notice that your attention has strayed elsewhere. Hard pushing or frantic pulling is not required to get your mind back in the present moment.

Anyone Can Learn to be Mindful: We all have the potential to pay attention or to be mindful in school and all of life, but very few of us have ever been shown how.

Essence of Meditation: Meditation is a basic practice to develop mindfulness. You don't *have* to meditate to be mindful, but it sure does help. Meditation is essentially sitting still and breathing naturally with full attention to sitting and breathing.

Steps in Meditation: Meditation involves (1) sitting and paying full attention to breathing; (2) noting when your mind has wandered; (3) simply observing without analysis or judgment that your mind has strayed; (4) letting go of whatever thoughts and emotions emerge; (5) gently allowing your mind to return to quiet sitting and breathing; and (6) beginning again, and again, and again...when your mind drifts from your breath in the present moment.

Scientific Support for the Benefits of Meditation: Scientific research primarily by neuroscientists and psychologists provides evidence that mindfulness meditation has a positive influence on learning in school, mental and physical health, brain functioning, sports, job satisfaction, and many other areas and activities.

Intellectual Understanding Is Not Enough: Mindfulness is easy to understand intellectually but difficult to consistently put into operation in your everyday life. It takes commitment, patience, and practice.

Avoid Self-judgment: Be kind to yourself. Develop self-compassion. When you think about your practice of mindfulness, it may seem that you aren't getting anywhere or you aren't doing it right. Just keep going without criticizing yourself. The effects are often subtle and cumulative. Just assume that they are occurring. There are no failures in meditation. You learn something and benefit every time you meditate.

Two Rules: The two primary rules of learning mindfulness are (1) begin, and (2) continue.

What you have just read may spawn doubts rather than wild enthusiasm. That's okay. Contrary to what you may expect, it's good even from our perspective. We want you to question everything we present. We want you to test our suggestions for yourself. Don't take our word for anything.

Even if you've just finished this section and you're thinking, "Nope. Not for me. I don't have the time or the interest for this." Please read on, if nothing else we hope to at least help shift your attitude toward learning, and, who knows, by the time you finish this short read, you may have decided to give mindfulness and meditation a try.

The book is laid out to provide a short background on mindfulness practice, personal stories containing relevant lessons, and some basic instruction for implementation. We urge you not to rush ahead. As you read, consider how what we say might fit into your life. When you read something you think may help you, give it a try.

Part I

The Art and Science of Paying Attention

Chapter 1

The Los Angeles Lakers and the Dalai Lama

What do members of the LA Lakers and the Dalai Lama have in common, besides, of course, name recognition and spiffy outfits?

They have extraordinary powers of attention and concentration, which they've enhanced through the practice of meditation. Everyone knows that the Dalai Lama practices meditation, but even most ardent basketball fans are surprised to find out that Phil Jackson, the coach who led the Chicago Bulls and the LA Lakers to a combined 11 NBA championships, hired a mindfulness meditation coach for his players. Coach Jackson has practiced meditation for many years, and mindfulness or full attention is an essential component of his coaching style and strategy. He has even written a book on his personal journey and his unique approach to coaching: *Sacred Hoops: Spiritual Lessons of a Hardwood Warrior.*[1]

As you'll see, the mindful approach to paying attention can be applied to many areas, including learning, and it's a better approach than what most of us use. The development of mindfulness or full attention through meditation has staying power. It's been around for centuries, and in the last two decades, there have been more and more scientific studies supporting the effectiveness of mindfulness practices.

The strategy for staying in the moment is that when negative or positive disruptive thoughts and emotions draw you away from what you're doing in the present, let them be without trying to push them away or make them stay, and gently let your mind return to what you are doing in the present.

This approach represents a far-reaching change in what most of us think is the best way to get where we want to go. The departure from the conventional view of devoting more attention to what we get for doing something (ends or goals) in relation to what we do to attain our goals (means or process) is a radical shift in how we see the world, and it can have a substantial impact on our ability to get things done.

Something to keep in mind in your journey through this book is that reading about how to pay attention is not enough. Reading just promotes intellectual understanding. You need practical understanding. You want to apply what you read to your daily life.

Let's consider an example: Say that you want to learn how to ride a bike. You read dozens of manuals on bike

---

1   Jackson and Delehanty, 1996

riding; you attended lectures by experts on how to ride a bike; and you watch videos of cyclists happily peddling along. If you carefully pay attention, this provides you with an idea of how to ride a bike. However, intellectual or book knowledge of how to ride a bike is not enough to learn how to actually ride. To ride a bike, you have to put your knowledge into practice. You have to get on a bike and ride it. You will experience fear, hesitation, wobbling, and perhaps crashing before you are eventually able to keep your balance. You'll have to practice braking, turning, and other skills that you've read about and watched before you become a competent bike rider. Without putting your intellectual understanding of bike riding into practice, you'll never experience the joy of riding.

Chapter 2

The Purposes and Effects of Meditation

This book started with a presentation of meditation among some of the best basketball players in the world and the most widely recognized contemporary spiritual leader. Many people who are not household names also practice mindfulness meditation for a variety of reasons. This section presents a brief review of the popularity, purposes, and effects of mindfulness meditation in a number of areas.

Mindfulness meditation is best known as a Buddhist spiritual practice that was introduced more than 2,500 years ago. It has been practiced by billions of people in a broad range of cultures and for a variety of reasons. Just considering its longevity suggests that it must have some positive effects.

In the last couple of decades, the practice of meditation has been applied to a wide variety of secular and practical activities. Modern research on the effects of the ancient practice of mindfulness meditation has shown us that it has some impressive results, including positive psychological and physiological effects. We'll see below that mindfulness meditation is useful in areas from brain functioning to business management. Most importantly for us is its application to learning. The wide applicability of mindfulness and the growing number of people who practice it is indicative of a mindfulness revolution taking place.[2]

The Military[3]

We'll begin our discussion with mindfulness in the U. S. Armed Forces because it's probably one of the most surprising applications of meditation. Mindfulness is practiced even among battle-hardened Marines. It has been endorsed by high ranking officers in the military, and has been found useful for both those being deployed to combat zones and those returning. Mindfulness meditation and related practices have been recommended for problems such as PTSD, severe stress, anxiety, self-destructive behavior, information overload, and cognitive difficulties.

The most well know mindfulness program in the military is Mindful-based Fitness Training (MMFT or M-fit). The purpose of the program is to prepare soldiers and Marines mentally through mindfulness practices to complement their physical fitness training.

---

2   For a succinct review of the effectiveness of mindfulness meditation see McCown, Reibel, and Micozzi, 2011

3   Campbell, 2011; Meditation, 2010; Ryan, 2012

Encouraged by the initial results of research on M-fit and acceptance among soldiers, both the Army and Marines are conducting experiments to further test the effectiveness of mindfulness meditation. It's been suggested that M-fit should be expanded and evaluated among police, firefighters, and others in stressful public service jobs.

Members of our Armed Services deserve effective treatment of mental health problems, for ethical and practical reasons. There are those in upper echelons of the military who have recommended the expansion of mindfulness practices in the Armed Services as a cost effective method for addressing a wide range of psychological problems.

Prison[4]

There are hundreds of organizations and individuals teaching meditation to thousands of inmates and staff members in correctional facilities. There are programs in a number of countries, including the U.S., U.K., and India. Meditation is even taught in prisons with reputations for violence and other problems.

A widely known organization teaching mindfulness practices in penal institutions is the Prison Mindfulness Institute. Its latest mindfulness-based program, *Path to Freedom*, involves participants while they are in prison and after their release. Researchers from Harvard, Brown, Rhode Island College, and the University of Rhode Island are members of the of the program team. Early results show reduced anxiety, violence, and prison rule violations, and increased emotional intelligence.

---

4   Prison Mindfulness Institute, Newsletter, October, 2010; Lozoff, 1985; Dhamma Brothers, 2007

In addition to mindfulness programs and research, there have been a number of self-help books written by prisoners on meditation, mindfulness, and other contemplative practices. One of the earliest and best known books of this genre is *We're All Doing Time* by the late Bo Lozoff. Films are also a vehicle for information on meditation among prisoners. *Dhamma Brothers* is an example of an award winning documentary on meditation in prison. The film was shot in one of the most violent maximum security prisons in Alabama.

Medicine[5]

Jon Kabat-Zinn can be credited with initiating and advancing the mindfulness movement in medicine. More than 30 years ago, Professor Kabat-Zinn developed mindfulness-based stress reduction (MBSR) at the University of Massachusetts Medical Center. MBSR has helped more than 16,000 patients to deal with the stress of serious illness, and it has been adopted by 250 medical centers in the United States. MSBR has been expanded to address problems and stress for people in a variety of environments. There are hundreds of research studies demonstrating that MBSR is effective in reducing pain, anxiety, stress, and depression, and in promoting successful coping strategies and healing.

Brain Functioning[6]

Until fairly recently, the view held by almost all neurologists was that the brain did not change much after a relatively early stage in growth and development. The conventional

5   University of Massachusetts Medical Center, 2006
6   Begley, 2007; Davidson, 2003; Hanson with Mendius, 2009

view was brain neurons were not generated and redistributed after the brain reached full maturity when individuals were in their 20's. This is no longer the prevailing view.

In the late 1990's, advances in measurement techniques and the efforts of brain researchers like Dr. Richard Davidson changed everything. There has been a radical shift in the view of the brain. Neuroplasticity or the brain's capacity to continue to develop and restructure throughout life is now the scientifically accepted view.

In the past decade or so, researchers at some of the most prestigious American universities and medical centers have studied meditation and the brain using the latest brain measurement techniques. The results of the research consistently demonstrate that meditation is among the best methods to improve brain structure and function throughout life. This is truly a breakthrough research finding.

Mental Health and Recovery[7]

There has been widespread growth in the application of mindfulness in the mental health field. Mindfulness-based practices have been successfully incorporated into mental health treatment programs that help people with problems ranging from mild and moderate psychological difficulties to debilitating psychiatric disorders.

Mindfulness-based stress reduction (MBSR) has become a model for a variety of approaches grounded in mindfulness. The range of mindfulness-based interventions (MBI's) has been rapidly expanding. Examples include: mindfulness-based cognitive therapy (MBCT), mindfulness-based trauma therapy (MBTT), mindful-

---

7   Linehan, 1991; Begley; 2007; McQuaid and Carmona; Alexander, 1997, McCown, Reible, and Micozzi, 2011

ness-based eating awareness training (MB-EAT), and mindfulness-based relationship enhancement (MBRE). Dialectical Behavioral Therapy (DBT) and Acceptance and Commitment Therapy (ACT) are examples of interventions that include mindfulness as a central component.

Team Sports[8]

As noted in the introduction of this book, mindfulness practice has even found its way into professional sports, a world of mega-salaries and gargantuan egos. The prime example is the effort of Phil Jackson, the most successful NBA coach in the history of professional basketball. Coach Jackson has practiced meditation for years and he has firsthand knowledge of its effects. In his book, *Sacred Hoops: Spiritual Lessons of a Hardwood Warrior*, Phil Jackson observes that there are great benefits for professional athletes in the practice of mindfulness:

"When players practice what is known as mindfulness – simply paying attention to what's actually happening – not only do they play better and win more, they also become more attuned with each other."

Professional basketball is not the only team sport where players have been taught to meditate. Mindfulness has been introduced into a wide range of sports in a variety of countries. For instance, the Caerphilly Rugby Club, a Welsh team that has been in existence for 117 years, has engaged a Buddhist monk to teach the team meditation as a way to enhance team performance. Meditation has also become a component of high school athletic programs. In his book, *Boyz to Buddhas*, David Forbes describes meditation as part of a program for high school football players.

---

8   Jackson and Delehanty, 1996; Wilson, 2004; Forbes, 2004

Fitness

Yoga and the martial arts are the classic examples of mindfulness practices as they're applied to fitness. However, a growing number of top fitness professionals like JC Deen (jcdfitness.com) and Leo Babauta, (zenhabits.net) have written articles and developed programs implementing aspects of mindfulness to help clients with everything from beginning an exercise routine to preparing for physique competitions.

Business[9]

Feature stories such as *"Zen and the Art of Corporate Productivity"* have appeared in Business Week and other popular magazines for the last ten years. The articles report that an increasing number of businesses are supporting meditation programs to reduce employee stress and increase productivity. Meditation instruction is one of the perks increasingly offered by businesses to attract and retain qualified employees and enhance their physical and psychological health at relatively low cost. Many corporate executives consider meditation programs an effective and relatively inexpensive way to reduce absenteeism and increase efficiency and creativity.

In 1996, working with corporations and other organizations to promote mindfulness and its benefits in the workplace became part of the mission of The Center for Contemplative Mind in Society (CCMS). Mirabai Bush, cofounder of CCMS, recalls that at first she was apprehensive about working with corporations, but her concern was quickly allayed. CEO's and employees were generally

---

9   Der Hovanesian, 2003; Cullen, 2006; Napoli, 2012

receptive to mindfulness and had no trouble recognizing its benefits. CCMS and Monsanto developed the first corporate mindfulness practices program in the U.S., and Google has been among CCMS' other partners. In 2008, a successful mindfulness-based emotional intelligence program was developed for Google employees.

In addition to Google, Hughes Aircraft, Deutshe Bank, Aetna, Merck, and General Mills are among the corporations that provide meditation classes for their employees. Meditation has also been introduced into business schools as part of educating future business leaders. For example, top ranked business programs such as the Harvard MBA Program offer courses in mindfulness meditation for their students.

Learning and Practicing Law[10]

Meditation instruction is offered for both students and professors at law schools, including Yale, Columbia, Harvard, and Berkeley. Also, attorneys in some firms have taken courses in mindfulness meditation and participate in meditation groups. Steven Keeva of the American Bar Association Journal published a book on incorporating meditation and other ways of developing attention or awareness into legal work, and articles on full attention or mindfulness and legal education have appeared in journals such as the Harvard Negotiation Law Review.

---

10   Graham 2006; Johnston, May 29, 2006; Kabat-Zinn, 2005; Keeva, 1999; Riskin, 2002

Government[11]

The broadest application of mindfulness is to the nation. The author of *A Mindful Nation*, Tim Ryan, is a veteran U.S. Representative of five terms. Among other duties, Congressman Ryan serves on the House Armed Services Committee and House Budget Committee. He is also co-chair of the Congressional Manufacturing Caucus. In other words, this guy is no slouch.

Congressman Ryan's work is comprehensive, cogent, and thoughtful. He provides a concise and readable review of the literature on mindfulness. In addition, he includes in his book dozens of interviews with experts and practitioners in mindfulness-based programs.

In his book, Representative Ryan describes the benefits of mindfulness in his personal life and the scientifically supported use of mindfulness for medicine, education, and many other areas. He argues that given that mindfulness has been proven to successfully address a number of problems related to these areas at a fraction of the cost of other approaches, it makes sense for the government to financially support programs based on meditation and mindfulness.

At a much more encompassing level, Tim Ryan proposes that some of the general characteristics developed as part of mindfulness and awareness can help to solve some of the broader more complex social and economic problems facing the U.S. The factors of compassion and spaciousness of mind associated with increasing levels of awareness can result in new ways to approach some of our most intractable problems.

---

11   Ryan, 2010

Higher Education[12]

The central topic of this book is, of course, mindful learning. For more than a century, a number of astute observers ranging from the influential 19th Century American philosopher, psychologist, and educator William James to Japanese Zen Master Yasutami have pointed out that incorporation of the process of paying attention or the development of mindfulness would be of great benefit to Western education.

More than 20 years ago, Dr. Ellen Langer of Harvard University was one of the first to give a book-length treatment to the application of the principles of mindfulness to learning with the publication of her book *The Power of Mindful Learning*. According to Professor Langer, some attention paid to mindfulness in our schools would promote student attention and interest, which would lead to better learning.

The findings reviewed on the uses and benefits of mindfulness practice are directly relevant to your life as a student. Schoolwork will go much better when you are feeling positive or your state of mind is favorable to learning. Everyone is sometimes taxed by the amount of work or the nature of assignments, and the ability to deal with such conditions without suffering debilitating mood decline is important for performing well in school and all of life.

Developing the ability to pay attention has received growing attention as an educational topic in recent years. The Association for Contemplative Mind in Higher Ed-

---

12   James, 1890; Kapleau, 1980; Langer, 1997; Association for Contemplative Mind in Higher Education, 2012; Center for Contemplative Mind in Society; Shapiro, Brown, and Astin, October 2008

ucation (ACMHE)[13], for instance, provides financial support and guidance to professors who are developing courses and programs to introduce students to contemplative practices, including mindfulness meditation. The courses designed by recipients of fellowships employ the practice of mindfulness as a way to promote deeper understanding and creativity. In addition to supporting course development, ACMHE disseminates information on mindfulness and other practices and offers courses and conferences for educators.

To date, more than 120 contemplative fellowships have been awarded to professors at over 80 colleges and universities. The program has provided support for course development to professors of literature, mathematics, art, philosophy, business, medicine, religion, music, dance, criminology, art, and many other disciplines. These professors teach in a wide variety of institutions ranging from large research universities to small liberal arts colleges.

Evidence supporting the incorporation of meditation and mindfulness into higher education is presented in the report *Toward the Integration of Meditation into Higher Education: A Review of the Research*. The report reviews and summarizes hundreds of studies on the use of meditation in higher education. The research studies included in the report have a combined sample of thousands of participants representing a wide range of students. Research subjects include undergraduate and graduate students in various disciplines and a relatively substantial number of medical students.

The findings of the report support the claim that meditation and mindfulness can have positive effects on

---

13   Association for Contemplative Mind in Higher Education. www.acmhe.org, 2013

learning. The results indicate that mindfulness can improve (1) meeting traditional academic objectives, such as grades and cognitive skills; (2) stress reduction and favorable psychological states; and (3) creativity, understanding of others, and compassion for self.[14]

14   Shapiro, Brown, & Astin, October 2008

Chapter 3

Meditation and Mind Development

Much of what was just presented on the influence of meditation on physiological and psychological health as well as its use for a variety of purposes represents what Lawrence LeShan considers the first of the two major results of meditation.[15]

As we have seen, mindfulness meditation enhances our ability to pay attention to what we are doing in the moment. This improves our ability to effectively and efficiently perform tasks. LeShan also points out that meditation has practical benefits because it increases our enthusiasm in everyday life by helping us deal with anxiety and other impediments to performance.

---

15   LeShan, 1974

The practical results of mindfulness documented in systematic studies and practical applications are for many of us reason enough to practice meditation. However, as LeShan notes, there is a second central result of meditation: we develop a higher level of consciousness or an expanded perspective on reality.

At higher stages of consciousness or mind, we generally have a broader view and see the world differently than at lower stages. The material world has not changed. What has changed is our perspective, the way we frame the world, or the way that we look at things. We have a different view ("fresh eyes") at higher levels than we do at lower stages. The great benefit of progress in stage of mind development is problems that were impenetrable at a lower level or stage can be solved at a higher level.

The Importance of Level of Human Consciousness or Mind Development[16]

Most experts on human development agree that the levels of human consciousness or mind are hierarchically arranged. Each of us can move under appropriate conditions from an infantile and self-centered view of our world to higher levels of mind such as the rational stage, and a relatively small number of people advance beyond the rational to transpersonal stages.

At the rational level of mind, human reason and abstract thinking emerge. Reason, including the scientific method and conceptual thought, has brought us unprecedented technological, medical, and scientific progress along with material wealth and political liberties. Industrial and post-industrial nations have reason at their core. Today, all

---

16   Wilber, 1995, 1997, 2000, 2002, and 2003

societies that are part of the global economy must have a critical mass of individuals and institutions operating at the rational level. Societies and individuals that operate at levels below the rational or modern are left behind.

Although the ability to think at the rational level is of great benefit, and everyone should develop the ability to use reason, most of the thinking done by people is not at the rational or modern level. Research shows that many of us do not think at the rational level most of the time. There is a small percentage of the population who think at high levels of rationality, however, most people in the world operate at a level that is a mix between low-level rationality and the stage below, which is a level characterized by concrete rather than abstract thinking.

Anything that can move us up in level of consciousness such as the practice of mindfulness meditation is important. Currently, on both the collective and individual level, we face serious challenges that require an increase in our individual and collective level of consciousness to adequately address. Just a few of our current difficulties include environmental degradation, economic failure, genocide, terrorism, international conflict, depression, anxiety, and adapting to an ever-increasing pace of economic, technological, social, and political change.

Research shows that meditation influences rationality. In one study, it was found that in comparison to non-meditators, those who meditated made more rational decisions when faced with a decision-making situation. MRI scans of the brain indicated that rational rather than emotional areas of the brain were engaged for meditators. It was just the opposite for their non-meditating counterparts.

It makes sense that mindfulness increases effectiveness in decision making. Those who are mindful are better at letting go of thoughts and feeling that are irrelevant to the decision than are those who do not practice mindfulness.

Rationality and Higher Education

Higher education should prepare students to adapt to life in the modern world, which is defined by reason and rational thought. Many leading thinkers consider raising student levels of rational thinking to be among the primary objectives of higher education.[17]

Rational thought used appropriately for rational ends is good for both individuals and society. The more people we have in the world at the rational stage of development and the higher the level of rationality they achieve, the better for all of us. As we move up in our level of mind, our perspective broadens, our compassion and concern deepens, and our problem-solving ability expands. More people reaching higher levels of rationality is also beneficial because attaining an adequate level of rationality is a necessary condition for moving on to even higher stages of consciousness. For example, the stage above the rational is called integrative logic, vision logic, or creative logic. In essence, it's the ability to truly comprehend and integrate multiple perspectives to develop better solutions.

Higher Consciousness, Higher Education, and Mindfulness

Because we can understand more and lead lives that are more meaningful at higher levels of mind, it seems reasonable to see our purpose in life as advancing along the spectrum of consciousness. It also seems reasonable that one

---

17   See, e.g., Nussbaum, 1997

of the purposes of higher education should be to assist students in progressing to their highest potential in mind development. This will benefit individuals and society.

Where does meditation practice fit into all of this? Mindfulness meditation helps us to develop our capacity to pay attention, which assists in learning no matter what we are trying to learn at any level. Most of the content we are required to learn in higher education in the modern world is the product of reason, and the methods for generating information and problem-solving we learn in most professional and academic disciplines are based on rational procedures and techniques. In other words, the methods and content of most of our education will reflect the rational level, and there is little doubt that increasing our mindfulness can help us learn better at this level.

Chapter 4

Now and Zen: The Confused Journey of a Zen Inept

Let's take a break from reviewing the first and second results of meditation and mindfulness to explore the reality of one man's long journey along the path of learning the importance and difficulty of paying attention. This is the story of the elder Gibbs, Jake. I'll tell you about my personal experience because (1) it's the one I know best, and (2) I'm the most interesting man in the galaxy, and it should be important to all beings (human and otherwise) that my story is told. I should note that my wife Kate, our daughter Sarah, and our son (and my coauthor) Roddy think I'm pretty boring. However, I do not consider them to operate at a level of consciousness at which they can judge me. Our dog, Lily Anne Whippet, thinks I'm fascinating.

The real reason I'm telling you my story is to encourage you to give mindfulness a try. If I learned to apply mindfulness, although admittedly my experience has been uneven, I contend anyone can learn to be more mindful or to pay attention better. You just have to keep coming back to it through your ups and downs.

A Birthday Wish

Many years ago on his birthday, I asked my friend, Marty Zakis, historian, philosopher, and Latvian hand-painted necktie enthusiast, his wish for the future. Marty replied, "Someday, just one (expletive deleted) time, I'd like to be where (expletive deleted) I am."

At the time, Marty's statement didn't make a lot of sense to me. You are always where you are; you can't be any place else. So why wish for it? Why didn't he wish for a girlfriend he didn't deserve to be in the same galaxy with? Why didn't he wish for free beer and hot dogs for life at O'Heany's Tavern? Why didn't he wish to inherit a medieval castle in Latvia, complete with serfs and a sculpture of the Maiden of Latvia Swimwear Competition Winner of 1343 AD?

Although I discounted Marty's birthday wish, his words stuck in my mind. I thought about them from time to time, and I gradually came to appreciate his wish. I realized I was never where I was. I was never fully present doing with complete attention whatever I was supposed to be doing. No matter where I was, my mind wasn't entirely there. Thoughts of other times and places intruded on the present with maddening regularity. My mind was constantly time sharing in the past, present, and future. My thoughts were always jumping all over the place. I was continually in a state of scattered mind.

Eventually, I wished I had never listened to Marty's wish. By occasionally observing my state of mind when I was supposedly involved in a task in the present, I realized just how uninvolved I was. When I was in class, I was thinking about what I would do when I got out of class or what I wished I could do. When I started on a trip, I was thinking about arriving at the destination. Even when I was having a great time, the depressing thought that eventually it would end would enter my consciousness. Of course, I was partially aware of the present, but I was never fully involved or fully absorbed in what I was doing in the present moment.

My observations of myself resulted in a deeper appreciation of the present. I reasoned that if the present was the only reality, and my life was important to me, I should try to live more in the present. I also realized that if I lived in the present, I would probably be better at things because my mind and mental energy would not be distributed among three time zones (past, present, and future). I might even enjoy more whatever I was doing at a particular time.

"Power to the present" became my motto. No more zoning out to the past and future. I would mentally superglue myself to the present. I would make myself a present of the present.

Time Wars

My initial attempt at staying in the present was an aggressive mind-over-time strategy. I resolved to push out the past and the future to capture all mental territory for the present, its rightful owner. No effort was too great.

My strategy backfired. I was outmaneuvered. Entire armies of thoughts and images from the future and the past invaded the present with overwhelming force. I was decisively defeated.

I was humiliated. I felt foolish for even trying to stop the juggernaut of intrusive past and future thoughts. What hubris on my part. After all, I am but one puny human being.

I returned to my old ways. I once again grew comfortable with the idea of entertaining a variety of thoughts and feelings associated with the past and future while I was acting in the present. It became second nature for me to multitask. I planned my day or reviewed events from the previous day while taking my morning shower. While sitting in class, I developed a rich fantasy life of romance, athletic accomplishments, and athletic romantic activities. When I sat down to study, my mind was stuck on how long it would be until I was finished.

I came to believe that this was the way things should be. It was a natural state for humans. It was familiar and comfortable. I concluded that my effort to stay only in the present had been misguided. I apologized to my mind for starting a civil war, and I returned to my comfortable old ways. I happily bounced from thought to thought, and I cheerfully endured being tugged this way and that with constantly changing mind states.

I called Marty Zakis to tell him of the foolhardiness of his birthday wish. He didn't remember making it. He then told me that he had recently discovered that he was a descendant of Medieval Latvian royalty. It turned out to be true. I'm not kidding. Honest to Buddha.

Frozen in Fear

The idea that it is better to be fully present than absent part of the time kept reemerging in my life. It was reinitiated following a scary incident in Newark, NJ, where I was working at the time. I was walking down Washington Street to meet some colleagues for lunch at the Garden Restaurant when a guy approached me and pulled out an enormous knife. From my perspective at the time, it looked like a samurai sword, and the guy wielding it appeared to have bad intentions. My initial reaction was to freeze in terror. This brilliant defensive move was followed by my turn-and-run gambit, a technique I had perfected shortly after entering kindergarten at St. Peter the Apostle School in Troy, NY.

A few days after the event when my heart stopped racing, but my mind had not, it occurred to me that if the menacing guy brandishing the knife had ever cornered me, I would have no idea of what to do. I fantasized about making several whirlwind moves and disarming my tormentor. I even thought of arming myself. Of course, the reality was if I possessed a firearm, I would be embarrassed in front of friends, family, students, and colleagues. I had been known on occasion to be an extraordinary windbag who could blo-viate for hours on the issue of gun control. Besides, if I had a gun I might shoot somebody, for instance, me.

What I thought was a reasonable solution emerged when I came across an advertisement to study self-defense at a local martial arts school. The words study and art ap-pealed to me. I figured I could learn to fly like the martial artists in the movies typically shown on TV on Saturday afternoons during the late 70's and early 80's. I was hop-ing that I might even be able to acquire the elocutionary technique favored by Kung Fu masters in early martial arts movies where the sounds of words are made several seconds after the movement of the lips. You would have to be insane to accost a man who could speak this way, even if he looked like me.

Unfortunately, I selected a martial arts school that emphasized physical conditioning and sparring over philosophy and esoteric techniques. I didn't learn the "death touch" or how to catch a bullet in my teeth, as I had hoped. Most of my training consisted of catching roundhouse kicks to the ribs. I also became quite adept at blocking punches with my face.

Kicked and Punched into the Past

I trained in Goju-ryu karate under the guidance of Sensei Ron Gaeta and Sensei Ken Post, a couple of "Jersey guys" whose idea of a good time was doing dozens of pushups followed by multiple rounds of sparring. When I moved from New Jersey to Pennsylvania, I trained in Judo and Taekwondo with Sensei Larry Driscoll who had a similar approach to my New Jersey instructors. While "studying" the "art," I became interested in the rich history of the martial arts, and I started reading about it. Not unexpectedly, I found that I was much better at reading about the martial arts than I was at fighting, and it didn't scare me nearly as much.

Ch'an

I learned from my reading that a form of Buddhism called Ch'an (breath) became a popular practice in China and it is still practiced today. The central teaching of Ch'an is that the best way to live life is to pay full attention. By completely attending to what is going on, we learn that life doesn't have to be as hard as we make it. The method is simply to devote complete attention to the present and experience what happens.

Bodhidharma, who brought the teachings of Buddha from India to China, developed the martial art of Kung Fu, which influenced the fighting arts of Japan and Korea. Bodhidharma had two purposes in mind in developing a martial art. Both were practical. One was to provide his unarmed monks with some way to defend themselves from highway robbers. The monks did not possess much, but they were easy targets.

The other purpose was to furnish an alternative to sitting meditation as a way of developing mindfulness or the ability to pay attention to the moment. Some monks were having trouble sitting for long hours in a cross-legged position simply paying full attention. As an alternative, they would practice martial art fighting movements in prearranged steps with total immersion or attention. It was a form of moving meditation.

Zen

Ch'an spread to Japan, where it thrived. Ch'an, which is pronounced Zen in Japanese, influenced many aspects of Japanese culture. Even today, Zen can be seen in Japanese forms of visual art, poetry, flower arranging, and gardening.

Zen has had a major influence on Japanese techniques of combat. One of its earliest applications was to the bow. Full concentration on shooting the arrow in the present rather than on the objective of hitting the target resulted in greater accuracy. The Zen way also became an integral part of unarmed martial arts such Karate do, Judo, and Aikido.

Moving Beyond Battle

I read many books on the modern unarmed forms of Japanese martial arts. The message in all that I read was the same: proper performance requires full attention to the present moment, and practice and discipline are essential. I learned, also, that Japanese martial arts are a way of life (do means way) that incorporate ethical principles, like respect and restraint.

My reading on the martial arts in which Zen was often central led me to read more about Zen. I learned that Zen is primarily considered a way of life to be applied right here and now. Indeed, Zen has been called the "art of life."[18] I found that in addition to the specific applications of Zen in Japan to rock gardening, art, and the tea ceremony, Zen has been suggested in the contemporary West as an approach to many activities: psychoanalysis; organizational management; social work; and driving a car. Zen has even been applied to Tango dancing, knitting, and falling in love.[19] It seems that the Zen approach can be applied to just about anything. If Zen is the art of life or paying full attention to what you are doing in the present, shouldn't it be applicable to everything you do in life? It should certainly be applicable to learning.

My interest in Zen Buddhism broadened to other forms of Buddhism and to meditation, mindfulness, and consciousness development. I found what I read compelling and useful. As I continued to read, my interest in full attention or mindfulness and meditation grew. I came to realize that in trying to implement my friend Marty's

---

18   Lissen, 1969

19   Fromm, Suzuki, and DeMartino, 1960; Low 1976; Brandon, 1976; Berger, 1988;. Park, 2004; Murphy, 2002; Shoshanna, 2005

birthday wish back in the day, I had used the wrong approach to being fully present. I didn't know *how* to pay attention. The way of learning to pay attention through meditation and its application to other areas of life, such as going to college, was very different from what I had used in my life up to that point.

Chapter 5

We All Know How to Pay Attention, Don't We?

The ability to pay attention has been recognized as important both by ancient masters of various wisdom traditions and by modern experts. When it comes to getting things done, it's doubtful that anyone would disagree that attention is essential. Just think of all the times in your life when parents, teachers, bosses, coaches, and others have implored you to just pay attention to what you are doing. You would think by now with all the attention paid to paying attention, we would be pretty good at it, but most of us are not. We are easily distracted from what we are doing in school and just about any other setting.

Is it that we don't try hard enough to pay attention? Or maybe activities like school just aren't interesting enough to hold our attention. Perhaps, we never learned a very effective method for paying attention, and our capacity for staying focused has not developed to its full potential.

Ask yourself if anyone has ever taught you how to pay attention. By this we mean a specific technique or set of instructions that you can practice like you would practice a sport, a dance, or a musical instrument. Can you describe the technique, method, or process you were taught for paying attention?

We've asked friends, students, and family members to respond to these questions. Very few have had anyone teach them a specific method for paying attention or improving their ability to focus on a task or activity. An even smaller number have consistently practiced a method when they have been taught one. The purpose of our book is to offer you help in this area.

But Aren't We Taught to Pay Attention in School?

It's not that we don't acquire any ability to pay attention in school. It is the way we learn to concentrate on schoolwork that is the problem. Obviously, we figure out something about how to pay attention in school or we wouldn't learn anything. However, we can learn how to pay attention much better than we do. Developing the ability to pay attention effectively requires some guidance and lots of practice. That's what this book is about.

Attention and Content in Education

The ability to learn the content of various disciplines along with their central methods of inquiry presupposes that you can pay attention long enough to learn. But teaching content and methods of inquiry alone does not help you learn to pay attention very well. Acquiring the ability to fully pay attention requires a method and way to practice it.

Paying attention fosters mindfulness or an awareness of what we are doing. Mindfulness requires presence. When we are mindful, we are conscious of what we are doing and center our attention on the process of doing it in the present moment. If we are inattentive or unaware, we are mindless. As Harvard professor, educator, and psychologist Dr. Ellen Langer sees it, much of our approach to learning in school, as well as other endeavors in life, reflects *mindlessness* rather than *mindfulness*. This limits our effectiveness, creativity, and satisfaction.[20]

Fighting for Attention

Although very few of us are taught a specific method for developing our ability to pay attention, most of us acquire a general approach to paying attention that is conveyed to us during our formative years by parents, teachers, and others.

The first major aspect of paying attention we learn from our prevailing culture is that it is necessary to keep our mind focused on what we'll get for our effort, i.e., reaching our goal and obtaining our reward. For example, it is assumed that the best approach to studying for an exam is to focus on getting a good grade and other benefits associated with academic success. It is thought that during test preparation at least some attention should be on our reward for doing well and this motivates us to study.

---

20   Langer, 1989 and 1997

The second aspect of paying attention we learn is an aggressive strategy to stay focused and keep our minds from wandering from what we are doing.

Common images students use to describe the kind of attention they pay to learn and perform well in school include phrases like "hit the books," "conquer material," "mind over matter," "smoke it," "nail it," "own it," "kick butt," "grind," "cram," "ground and pound," and "beat the books." One young woman reported that one of her friends, a male, characterizes vigorous studying as "making that book my bitch."

Forced Concentration or Rambo Hits the Books

Many people endorse forced concentration as the preferred method of paying attention. It's an aggressive stance like combat, war, or Rambo style.[21] Paying attention is seen as winning a war against distractions and asserting control over our unruly minds.

In the forced concentration or the combat model of attention, focus on everything from hitting a baseball to studying in school is a brain-smoking, mind-knuckling ordeal in which you are forced to subdue your foe with a demonstration of superior force. Putting your mind to learning is hardly a tender affair from this perspective.

Even if the war model were the best way to go about learning, nobody ever gives us detailed instructions on how to go about it. We are told to "try hard," "make the effort," "be aggressive," "bear down," "keep in mind what's at stake," and so on. However, we are seldom given specific instructions, methods, techniques that lead to paying attention in this way.

21   Fellman, 1998

Don't despair. There is an alternative to the war model or Fighting With Your Books (FWB). It's called Dancing With Your Books (DWB). You're probably not totally surprised by this given the subtitle of this book.

Chapter  6

Dancing With Your Books

A central objective of this book is to present you with a different way of framing, approaching, or looking at schoolwork and anything else you might do. Seeing things differently or exploring a new perspective is often a first step in doing things differently. It is frequently the most important step.

Our own educational pursuits have convinced us that the way we commonly look at learning is counterproductive. There have been alternative approaches around for centuries. But most of us ignore them or reject them for the more conventional approach to paying attention, i.e., the combat model or Fighting With Your Books (FWB).

There is no need to fight with your books or your mind. They are not something "out there" posing a threat that you must conquer or subdue to achieve your goals. The books are not your enemy.

A more productive and gratifying way to frame your relationship with your books is as dance partners. Dancing With Your Books (DWB) certainly brings up a different set of images than "making that book my bitch."

When you watch accomplished ballroom dancers, for instance, two become one in the act of dancing. There is no separation. They certainly don't fight with each other. If you faithfully follow the steps presented in this book, you can learn to dance with your books rather than fight with them. Of course, as every dancer knows, attaining proficiency is demanding work that requires motivation, patience, flexibility, persistence, and endurance.

Getting Out of Your Own Way

Truly learning to dance with your books requires that you develop the ability to focus on the task of learning or the dance itself without constantly shifting your attention to the results of your effort. Thinking about yourself while dancing, including status and other rewards of dancing well, gets in the way or interferes with your performance. It takes your attention away from the activity of dancing. Although it might sound bizarre at first, one of the major problems you face in learning to dance (or to do anything well) is to simply get out of your own way so that your attention is on learning. Learning to dance with your books or do anything else right requires that you become less self-centered and results-focused and more task-centered or process-focused.

Great professional dancers become fully absorbed or completely immersed in dancing when they dance. Many dancers, and other performers (e.g., professional athletes), will tell you that they perform best if there is only the performance when they perform. If they start thinking of themselves performing or people reacting to their performance, it interrupts their rhythm and takes them out of their flow. This doesn't mean that they are unconcerned with performing well or that they don't desire the benefits of successful performances such as money, recognition, and career advancement. It means that the best way to get the rewards as a result of dancing well is to pay attention to the dance itself while dancing.

Time-Place Dissonance

Another view of focusing on results is that it can cause time-place dissonance or an imbalance between means and ends or process and goals. Here's how it works: If while you are doing schoolwork and you pay attention mostly to the result that you hope to get, which is by definition in the future, it takes your attention away from your involvement in your schoolwork or other activities, which are in the present. The only place you can perform an activity is in the present. Time-place dissonance occurs when the activity you are supposed to perform is in the present, but your mind is on the future, where you will receive the potential return on your investment of effort.

The Pervasiveness of Process-Goals or Means-Ends Imbalance

As we have pointed out, most of us are very familiar with focusing on ends or external rewards like money, recognition, winning, and grades. We do this at the expense of the means, process, or activity, i.e., the *doing* itself. Just about everyone can recall a vivid example from their youth of the cost of focusing on results.

We all have memories of dance performances, music recitals, spelling bees, and/or organized sporting events where all we could think of was doing well and/or avoiding failure. Our focus was almost exclusively on getting positive recognition in the eyes of our parents, teachers, coaches, and peers and avoiding negative status because of a poor performance.

Go back to those days and remember how you felt. We'll use the example of Melvin M. Milquetoast, a kid who suffered from disappointing performances during his career in the White Dove Little League. Some of it was due to his lifelong tendency toward anxiety and his mediocre athletic ability. But a lot of it stemmed from his desire to look good or, more accurately, to avoid looking bad. It was the potential or future consequences of his performance that interfered with his ability to play.

Melvin felt pressure to perform well for his dad, his coach, and McLaughlin's Funeral Home, his team. His performance, especially when his dad was in the stands, was foremost in his mind. Invariably, he let down his team and his dad was humiliated.

When Melvin was just playing sandlot or pickup baseball with his friends, he felt less pressure, performed better, and had a lot more fun. He was more focused on the game itself.

It's too bad that Melvin didn't have a coach like John McCarthy, a former college and professional baseball player, who runs a baseball program for kids to teach them to focus on playing the game rather than on results. Coach Mac tries to replicate for his players the conditions he experienced as a kid when he played baseball with his friends just for the fun of it, for the love of the game. As he describes his approach, "I want full effort, but I won't keep score. And there are no trophies here. The reward here is the satisfaction of playing baseball." McCarthy wants his players to fully experience playing by settling into the moment. He teaches his kids to pay attention to the process of playing the game rather than to focus on winning and impressing others. Coach Mac observes, "I think when you're centered and still, it allows you to see the ball travel, to see the play unfold. You can be present to play and compete."[22] It sounds like mindful baseball to us.

Taking the Fun Out of It

Long ago and far away, there were three boys enrolled in St. Jude Thaddeus Grammar School: Georgie Foley, Dickie Quinn, and Georgie Thompson. Like most ten-year old guys, they immensely enjoyed the practice of harassing young girls and old men. Each day after school, they would bother a few of their female classmates as a warm-up and then move on to use their best techniques on Old Man Johnson.

Dr. Robert P. Johnson was a retired distinguished professor emeritus from a prestigious university and one of the crankiest old men in Cohoes, NY, a city made famous by its leading citizen, the science fiction writer Kilgore Trout.

Professor Johnson liked to stay active by reading academic tomes and writing his memoir on his front porch when the weather permitted. He could also be found walking his dog, Ignatius; tending to his garden in the summer; shoveling snow in the winter; or doing some other chores around the house.

---

22   McCarthy quoted in Aubrey, July 6, 2006

The boys found Old Man Johnson to be an especially rewarding victim because he was so reactive. He was easy to provoke to anger, which would quickly escalate into rage and continue to amplify. He would become so frustrated and furious that he would scream strings of epithets at the boys and command Ignatius to attack. Invariably, Ignatius ignored him.

One December afternoon just after loosening up by demolishing a snow replica of Saint Bertha of Blangy built in the schoolyard by the girls, the boys arrived at Old Man Johnson's armed with a half dozen snowballs each. "Before you start," said Professor Johnson, "I'd like to pay each of you a quarter for harassing me. You boys have been putting in a lot of time and effort. You've been doing a splendid job, and you deserve something for it." The boys were surprised and delighted.

The next day the boys enthusiastically arrived at the usual time, and with visions of quarters pumping great quantities of serotonin into their brains. Before they started to pester Old Man Johnson, he mentioned that Ignatius needed an expensive prefrontal lobotomy for chronic depression, and he could only afford to pay them 15 cents that day. The boys agreed to work for a lower wage, and they managed to put in an energetic effort.

The following day, Old Man Johnson announced that as long as Ignatius was going in for surgery, he decided he would get the limbic part of his brain surgically altered in the hope that it would help with his chronic agitation. Because of the additional medical expense, he would only be able to pay the boys a dime each. The boys were dejected and angry. Dickie Quinn, the brains of the outfit, called a meeting. As far as the boys were concerned, they had been putting in an honest effort and deserved at least 15 cents each for their work.

No matter what the state of Old Man Johnson's finances, the boys considered it a grievous affront to offer them anything less than 15 cents. Even if he had to go into debt to pay them, he should do it rather than to make an insultingly low offer. The boys concluded that an offer of 10 cents just wasn't worth their effort.

The boys emphatically rejected Dr. Johnson's offer. They pointed out to him that it would have long-term consequences in that they would never harass him again at any price. They would also discourage everyone they knew from bothering him.

Professor Johnson made a disingenuous apology to the boys. He asked them to reconsider. But they stood united and firm. They never again even blew a snow flake in his direction.

What happened here? How is it that something that brought the boys such enjoyment became something that they would not do unless they were compensated at a certain level? Where did the joy, excitement, and fun go? Professor Johnson turned lemonade into lemons (pardon the cliché). He took something that was a sweet time for the boys and transformed it into a sour experience. Sometimes we do this to ourselves, and it has implications for school, work, and everything else in life.

Implications for the Focus of Attention

Professor Johnson's strategy was to shift the focus of the boys' attention. He successfully moved their interest from the satisfaction of the activity itself to the money he paid them for doing it.

The fun and excitement of bothering Dr. Johnson is known as intrinsic, internal, or inherent reward or satisfaction. The financial reward associated with harassing him represents extrinsic, external, or instrumental reward or satisfaction. Professor Johnson managed to shift the context of what the boys were doing, and it changed the meaning of the activity for the boys. Remember, before he started paying the boys, their only reason for harassing the old man was that they found it enjoyable. The reward or satisfaction of harassing Old Man Johnson was an inherent, intrinsic, or natural part of the activity itself.

Money was not a built-in reward or part of the essence of the activity. The payment only became associated with the harassment because it was added on by Professor Johnson. Once the boys started to receive payment for harassing Old Man Johnson, they were getting something *for* doing the activity in addition to what they were getting *from* just doing it. Eventually, the money overshadowed the joy of doing, it became more important.

By introducing money, Dr. Johnson reframed the situation for the boys. He was able to neutralize the natural pleasure that they had found in the activity itself. The money changed their focus from the value of the activity itself (i.e., fun) to what they were going to get for performing the activity (i.e., money). Old Man Johnson had transformed what was once play into work.

The Lesson to Be Learned

What has been presented so far indicates that if you get too focused on external rewards or extrinsic satisfaction, you take attention away from what you are doing. Consequently, the intrinsic, internal, or inherent satisfaction of the activity (i.e., the reward from the doing in the moment) loses significance for you.

If external rewards, results, or outcomes associated with what you are doing are all that you can see, you are blind to the value in the activity itself. If the activity becomes devalued, you will pay less attention to it, and it's less likely that you will perform well.

In school, too much attention on grades, status, recognition, and the marketability of your degree can take your attention away from the process or joy of learning. It's not that grades and other extrinsic rewards are unimportant; they are of great significance to just about everyone. The problem is that emphasis on these external rewards when you're supposed to be fully involved in activities to achieve them can backfire. Focus on goals, objectives, or future rewards can actually reduce your chances of realizing them by taking your attention away from what you're doing (studying for a test or writing a paper, for example).

Chapter 7

Qualifying External Rewards and Results

As we've noted, extrinsic rewards or instrumental goals are important. They often satisfy essential needs and provide the initial motivation for working or doing anything else.

As we'll see in many different contexts presented in this book, the best way to acquire material wealth and other extrinsic objectives and rewards is to pay attention to what you have to *do* to get them. As we've noted several times, this way it's possible to get the intrinsic or inherent satisfaction *from* what you're doing in the present and the extrinsic or instrumental satisfaction in the future *for* doing it.

We want to emphasize again that external or instrumental rewards or future objectives are not the problem. Putting too much attention on them at the wrong time is the concern.

Support for the Process-Centered Approach and Intrinsic Satisfaction

A number of research studies on the effects of intrinsic and extrinsic rewards have been done with participants ranging from preschool children to college students and beyond to adults in the workforce. The research demonstrates that intrinsic rewards are more influential than extrinsic rewards in promoting performance, enthusiasm, creativity, and a sense of personal control.[23] In other words, a process orientation or focus on means is more important than a results orientation or focus on ends.

Robert I. Sutton, a professor of management science and engineering at Stanford University, reports that studies of innovation and creativity in product development teams show that more intrinsically focused groups are more successful in creating fresh and imaginative products than are extrinsically centered groups.[24] Teresa Amabile, a creativity researcher, calls it the "Intrinsic Motivation Principle of Creativity." Her research demonstrates that "...people will be most creative when they feel motivated primarily by interest, satisfaction, and challenge of the work itself – and not by external pressure."[25]

The Place of Goals, Outcomes, and Extrinsic Rewards

Establishing goals sets a course for where you want to be in the future. Specific outcomes or results are what you hope

---

23   Kohn, 1993; see also Csikszentmihalyi, 1990; Langer, 1989; and Ryan, Sheldon, Kasser, and Deci, 1995

24   Sutton, 2002

25   Amabile quoted in Sutton, 2002, p. 135

to find when you get there. Goals, objectives, dreams, and hopes shape and give meaning to what you choose to do.

Where you want to go and what you want to get should have a strong influence on your actions in the present. Your goals shape the focus and intensity of your attention and your sense of self.[26] Someone who wants to be a professional musician will concentrate on different activities than someone who wants to be a chemical engineer. Selecting an interesting and challenging goal is motivating and helps you focus your attention on what you need to do to accomplish your goal. However, as we previously explained, learning to pay attention fully or to work mindfully in the present helps you both to accomplish your goals and experience intrinsic satisfaction while you're doing it.

The Ancient Roots of Process or Task Focus

Scientific research showing the effectiveness of a process-centered approach or intrinsic orientation is relatively recent, but the perspective itself as a recommended way to do any task and more broadly as an approach to life has been around for centuries. In Buddhist traditions, it is known as Right Effort. The definition of Right Effort presented in this book is a secular (not religious) interpretation applied to learning.[27]

26 Csikszentmihalyi, 1997

27 A common presentation of Right or Wise Effort (also known as Right Diligence) in the Buddhist literature is as the endeavor to create wholesome qualities and eliminate unwholesome qualities in the service of reducing suffering, which is the essence of Buddha's teaching. The Mindful Way To Study focuses in part on an adaptation of two steps of the Path for secular purposes for staying in the present moment, i.e., effectively accomplishing schoolwork. Here "unwholesome qualities" would be anything that takes us from the present moment and what we are doing. "Wholesome qualities" are anything that keeps us in touch with what we are doing or an intrinsic

Buddha taught what he considered the best way to live. He developed a program, called the Eightfold Path, which was designed to reduce self-imposed difficulties and increase satisfaction in all that we do. The practices he taught have been tested in an experiential way by millions of individuals and examined in scientific studies by psychologists and neuroscientists. The results are clear: it's best to stay anchored in the present where life's difficulties and joys are experienced. This requires knowledge (insight) into how your mind operates and methods to help your mind work for you rather than against you. The aspects of Buddha's teachings presented in this book to reduce stress, enhance satisfaction, and promote effectiveness in learning can be considered applied psychology or a human development program.

All the steps in the Eightfold Path are called "Right." Used in this context, "Right" does not mean just or righteous. It means appropriate, effective, or wise.[28] Right or Wise Effort is one of the two steps of Buddha's program that we think are most relevant to people living in today's world. The other, Right Meditation, principally concerns learning to place your attention on the present moment by simply sitting and observing your mind.

The practices of Right Effort and Right Meditation help us be where we are or to stay in the present moment. They are about paying full attention to what we are supposed to be doing this moment, e.g., studying when we study or sitting when we sit.

---

focus. Right Effort along with Right Meditation promotes Right Mindfulness, which is the ability to stay in the present moment or awareness. Our secular view of Right Effort appears to have some commonality with more broadly applicable, spiritual definitions (see Salzberg, 1997, p. 168).

28 Kabat-Zinn, 2005

You Can't Force Right Effort

Right Effort and related terms such as process-centered approach, intrinsic orientation, flow, task-focus, and absorption in the moment are concerned principally with the focus of your attention. We already know the benefits of paying attention to the present moment and what we are doing. Understanding this is the easy part. The hard part is the act of actually focusing on the object of attention, which is right now doing just what we are doing. We must know and practice a method of keeping our attention on the present moment or focusing on what we are doing.

As discussed previously, it's common to try to force our attention on a task or to push our way into the present. This aggressive approach characterized by constant and forceful effort is sure to backfire. You can take our word for it. We are personally very familiar with this misguided strategy.

Here's an example of wrong effort or trying to force yourself not to think of the past or future so that you are only in the present. Imagine someone assigns you the task of not thinking of the number 5. You'll find that if you try to bully your mind not to think of 5, it will stick in your mind. Constantly, thinking about *not thinking* about the number 5, causes you to think about 5 constantly. Your effort not to think about 5 results in exactly what you don't want to think about.

The idea of finger cuffs is another way that may help you understand the power of intrusive thoughts in capturing your attention and keeping you from focusing fully on what you are doing in the present. The device consists of a small, woven straw tube. If you put a finger from each hand in opposite ends of the tube and try to extract your fingers by pulling, the tube becomes tighter around your fingers. The harder you pull, the tighter it gets. The device transforms your own effort to extract yourself into keeping your fingers prisoner. This is similar to trying to get free of intrusive thoughts by attempts to pull away from them. The harder you pull or the more you try to remove them, the more control they have over you.

A better way than forcefully trying to attend to the present or pushing out past and future thoughts is to adopt an accepting frame of mind that allows you to relax or settle into the moment. When you become aware of thoughts and feelings that are not directly relevant to the task at hand, note them without judging them, and gently let them be. Eventually, they will pass. Your mind will let them go.

Right Effort in School

While attending college, you have to focus on academic activities or tasks to attain your goal of a college degree. To reach your objective, it is a great help to learn to pay attention using an effective method. As suggested earlier, FWB (fighting with your books) isn't it. DWB (dancing with your books), the process-oriented approach or learning with Right Effort, is a much better bet.

For many students, assignments are not ranked among the most compelling of activities available. There are many interesting and enjoyable activities competing for attention. When you sit down to study for an exam, write a paper, or complete an assignment, you'll often find that you would like to be elsewhere doing something else. Sometimes you would rather be just about anywhere else doing just about anything else.

Schoolwork can be tough. It's often tempting to put off assignments. You sometimes think that if you put off what you have to do, you'll have more energy, interest, and motivation to get through it at a later time. You postpone as long as possible because you think what you anticipate will be at best uninteresting and at worst agonizing. But the task or assignment doesn't go away. You have to do it despite your objections. If you want an education you have to do the work. It takes effort. There's plenty of evidence that Right Effort is the best kind of effort to use.

Chapter 8

Right Meditation

R ight Meditation is the other aspect of Buddha's program for sensible living that is the most relevant for learning. Meditation is the essential practice for learning to be mindful. One of the most widely used definitions of mindfulness is "...paying attention in a particular way: on purpose, in the present moment, and nonjudgmentally."[29]

In conjunction with cultivating mindfulness, meditation is a way of observing our own minds to see what's going on and learning to keep our minds less cluttered and on task. One way to look at meditation is as the application of Right Effort to the deceptively simple activity of just sitting and breathing. Meditation is a way of mind training and development; it helps us become aware, attentive, or mindful of all that is happening. It is the prac-

---

29   Kabat-Zinn, 1994, p. 4

tice of learning to cope with mental and emotional impediments so that we can do what we need to do. Meditation results in a quieting of the mind and the development of a different perspective that helps us see more clearly what's going on in our interior lives. The process of meditation changes how we experience the world and it can lead to insights that can help us work, play, and relate to others in more meaningful ways.

Meditation: Purpose

For you, the immediate purpose of meditation is to make you a more effective student. Because meditation has been shown to improve brain functioning, diminish negative emotions and moods, increase focus, and enhance positive mental states, it obviously creates a favorable state of mind for learning.

Although meditation is a purposeful activity in that you want to attain your goals by achieving a state of presence in the moment, you should not be concerned with the purpose of meditation while you are meditating. While meditating, you guide your attention to the main activity of the moment, which in the initial practice is just sitting and breathing. Here you are using the breath as an object of meditation. Thoughts of why you are meditating, how well you are meditating, and what you are getting from meditating will arise. When you become aware of them, note that they are present, let them pass, and gently return to observing your breath. As you can see, you are essentially following the procedure previously described for doing a task with Right Effort.

How to Begin: The Three Elements of Meditation

It has already established that the widely practiced, conventional method of paying attention is not very effective. Brain-squeezing and a tense, aggressive focus on results to generate good performance is unproductive.

We've seen that an alternative to FWB or the Rambo model is needed, a different way is DWB or mindful learning. It is the application of Right Effort to school work. It's an intrinsic orientation or process-centered approach. The question that remains is precisely how to learn the alternative approach or mindfulness.

The sections that follow turn our attention to this question. Much of what has been presented earlier is of central relevance to learning mindfulness meditation. It warrants a second look to help us to understand the process of meditation.

The presentation of the essentials of meditation is organized into three related elements: posture, breathing, and attitude of mind.[30]

Start your practice as soon as you have finished reading these sections. Once you start, keep at it. Remember, meditation initiates you into mindfulness and Right Effort; it is your primary practice. It deserves and requires a commitment of time and effort.

Element 1: Posture

Flopping down in your favorite overstuffed chair and hanging your legs over an arm may be relaxing, but it is not a good position for meditation practice.

---

30   Deshimauru,1982

The positions described below are designed for the long haul. Humans have practiced these positions for centuries. They allow you to sit still for relatively long periods of time. We're not claiming that there is no discomfort in these meditation positions. However, for sitting very still, alert, and relaxed, you can't beat them.

Several sitting positions can be taken for meditation. Different postures are taught in different traditions. Two popular ways of sitting to practice mindfulness meditation are presented below.

The Indian or Tailor Position

Probably the most popular meditation position in the West is cross-legged sitting known as tailor, Indian, or Burmese. The position requires that you sit on the floor with one leg in front of the other. Both knees should stay below the hips and touch the ground, if possible. Sitting on a small firm cushion is usually needed to provide the elevation required to touch your knees to the ground and keep your spine straight. A flat cushion, mat, or rug is usually placed under the sitting cushion to lessen stress on the legs, feet, and knees. If you cannot touch your knees to the mat, use small pillows or cushions to support your knees.

Zufu and zabuton (Japanese words) are the terms usually used for the sitting cushion and flat cushion, respectively. You can purchase them, or you can also improvise: Use a couch cushion for a zafu and a folded blanket for a zabuton.

Sitting in a Chair

A regular chair can be used for meditation. A straight-backed kitchen chair is a good choice. When you are using a chair, try not to allow your back to rest on the back of the chair. Sit on the front half of the chair; keep your feet flat on the floor; and keep your back straight.

If it's difficult for you to sit on the front of the chair without your back touching the backside of the chair for support, don't worry about it. Put a cushion between your back and the back of the chair. Your state of mind not your posture is most important while sitting.

For descriptions of more mediation positions (kneeling, half-lotus, and full-lotus) see www.mindfulwaytostudy.com.

Sit Like a Baby

Most meditation teachers who have written about posture emphasize the importance of keeping your back straight while sitting. One Zen teacher[31] suggests a one-year-old child as a model for correct meditation posture. The baby sits up straight with her belly sticking out in front and her butt sticking out at the other end. This gives a slight curvature to the spine at the waist and keeps the upper body straight but relaxed.

When sitting, your head should be straight as if you are holding up the sky with the back of the top of your head. This will keep your chin in, your ears in line with your relaxed shoulders, and your nose and navel in line.

If the recommendations on posture don't suit you for medical or other reasons, just find a posture that does suit you. The same is true for all of the suggestions below.

Eyes, Mouth, and Hands

In many meditation traditions there are instructions on what to do with your eyes, mouth, and hands.

31   Aitken, 1982

Eyes: You can keep your eyes open and unfocused. Gaze about three feet in front of you, but do not look at anything in particular. There are some meditation traditions in which the eyes are closed. You can follow this custom if you like. It may be the way to go if you find yourself distracted by visual stimuli when you meditate.

Mouth: Some meditation teachers give instructions on what to do with your mouth and tongue during meditation. It's obviously not a good idea to chew gum, unless your meditation practice is mindful gum chewing. One set of instructions, often seen in the Zen literature, is your mouth should be closed, and your tongue should rest gently on the back of your upper front teeth or the front of the roof of your mouth.

Hands: The most common instruction for hand position is simply to let them rest on your thighs. There are other more detailed and complex positions, usually taught in Zen meditation or *zazen.* If you're interested in instruction in Zen hand position, *mudra,* see the additional information presented in www.mindfulwaytostudy.com.

Use a Posture that Works for You

Assuming a good posture is a way to pay respect to the practice of meditation. It can also help you develop and maintain the right attitude of mind while meditating.

Despite the helpfulness of sitting position, don't fret about the specifics of how you sit and criticize yourself for what you consider sitting errors. Do some experimenting on the best meditation position for you. Developing the mental quality of alert attentiveness is more important than details of sitting posture. Don't let your sagging shoulders and bending spine, for example, get in your way.

When Sitting Meditation Just Isn't An Option

There may be times (perhaps all of the time) when you are incapable of sitting meditation. You may have physical problems that preclude sitting. Some people who suffer from certain psychological/emotional problems may be too agitated to sit. Yet, the practice of mindfulness is important because it is an intervention that is effective with even severe psychiatric disturbances.[32]

If you are unable to practice sitting meditation, don't despair. You can practice walking meditation as an alternative. One way to do walking meditation is to follow the instructions on mindfulness meditation presented below, and mindfully walk in a circle or back and forth in a straight line.

Whatever meditation posture you adopt, what's most important is to remember to follow the general instructions for mindfulness practice: (1) notice that your mind has wandered, and (2) tenderly allow your mind to return to the present moment.

Place and Time

Once you have the knowledge and simple gear required to begin your meditation practice, the question arises of when and where to do it. The broadest answer is to do it wherever you can.

Select the setting where there are the fewest distractions and the smallest likelihood of being interrupted. If you have a quiet, private place where you live, designate it for meditation, if possible. Discreet walking mediation in the book stacks of the library is a fine alternative, if it's your only option.

---

32   Lineham, Hubert, Suarez, and Heard, 1991

When you start your daily meditation practice, sit for short periods of time. Three to ten minutes is plenty. You can increase the time that you meditate in increments of one minute until you reach 20 minutes. You may eventually sit for 45 minutes or more if you like. You can also meditate more than once a day. You can experiment with meditating for several consecutive sittings alternating each sitting with walking meditation. No matter what the length of your meditation, the most important aspects are your commitment and Right Effort.

When you first begin to practice meditation, and even after you have been practicing for years, you may find yourself wondering how much time has passed as you sit. Thoughts about time can be especially bothersome if you do your time keeping with a conventional watch or clock, which you have to look at to see the time. You are much better off if you use some kind of timepiece that you can set to alert you when the session has ended. A soft ringing watch or cell phone alarm is probably your best option to take care of time.

It's unlikely that a device that keeps time for you will completely eliminate thoughts about time, including a strong desire for the meditation period to end. These distractions will continue to occur frequently. When they come into consciousness, note them, let them pass, and allow your attention to return to sitting.

Schedule your daily meditation for any time you can conveniently fit it in. Make it a priority. Many teachers suggest the morning as the best time if you are only able to do one sitting. Begin your day with the application of Right Effort to sitting and breathing. Make a commitment to extend the Right Effort practiced in meditation to everything that you do, it's a good way to start your day.

Element 2: Breathing

The second element of meditation is breathing. Breath is essential for life and central to meditation in all Buddhist traditions. Breath is so important that some traditions are simply called breath. You'll recall that Ch'an means breath in Chinese and Zen is breath in Japanese.

The instructions for breathing in mindfulness meditation are simple: Breathe naturally in and out. You can focus on just about any part of the body when breathing. One common place is to feel air flow in and out through your nose. Another is to feel your belly rise and fall as you breathe in and out. In your meditation, you can focus on your breathing wherever you experience it most in your body.

Your breath is the object of your meditation, and breathing is all that you are doing in the present moment. To stay in the moment or the Now is a matter of observing your breath going in and out over and over again. The practice of mindfulness is to realize when your mind has strayed from the present (breathing) and has settled on thoughts, feelings, and/or sensations of the past and/or future. When you recognize where your mind has wandered, invite your awareness back to the breath.

Don't try to control your breathing. Don't try to breathe in any special way. Simply breathe in and breathe out. If your breath happens to be smooth and rhythmic during a particular meditation session, breathe smoothly and rhythmically. If your breathing is a bit ragged, breathe that way. Just settle into the way you're breathing. Don't try to change it, but don't try to maintain it, either. Just accept whatever your breathing is in the moment.

Counting Breaths

A basic and common form of meditation is breath counting. Simply count your breaths on the exhalation up to ten, and then begin over again. If you lose count, which you will do plenty of times, start over again. Be sure that you don't try to estimate where you are in the sequence of breath counting when your mind strays and you don't know what breath you're on. Just begin again at breath number one. It's not a failure to lose track of your breaths. There are no failures in meditation. Everything that arises during meditation is an opportunity to practice mindfulness.

The purpose of counting your breaths is not to get to ten or bust. You are simply using your own breath as the object of meditation. Just observe, watch, or follow your breath. Allow yourself to settle into whatever happens to be the state of your breathing, and let your attention rest there.

Breath Meditation Without Counting

The other form of breath meditation is following the breath without counting. The practice consists of breathing in and out noting when your mind has wandered from the breath. When you recognize that you have strayed, allow your mind to return to just breathing. Remember, just observe or note where your mind has roamed and let it come back to the breath.

Your job in meditation is to become absorbed in your breath one breath at a time. You observe and experience one breath and then the next. You sink into it. You witness it. You allow the breath to be the focus or object of your attention. You welcome the breath and surrender to it. But you don't try to manipulate your breath or mind into a particular place.

Start by counting three deep breaths, but then sit following the breath immersing yourself in the present. Accept and mindfully observe or witness anything that arises. Don't try to make anything that comes up stay if it's pleasant. Don't try to make it go away if it's unpleasant. Fully experience boredom, bliss, anger, contentment, anxiety, hatred, lust, or whatever comes up. Look at it or lightly touch it, but don't try to push it away, hold on to it, or analyze it. Watch it dissolve in its time. Be kind to it, and tenderly let your attention return to your breath.

Your mind has the capacity to observe your thoughts, feelings, and sensations without judging them or analyzing them. It's a matter of mind observing mind. The capacity to look without evaluating what is happening in your interior world develops with meditation practice and increases your level of awareness or mindfulness. It enhances your ability to quiet your mind and stay present. It's a method of improving your process orientation, or Right Effort.

Labeling

A technique that is used in conjunction with breath meditation is labeling thoughts, emotions, and sensations as they arise. It is a structured way of noting where your mind has wandered and reminding yourself to return to the breath.

Here's an example of labeling: Say that anxiety about an upcoming test emerges while you are meditating. Simply note without judgment that anxiety has arrived. You are just announcing the emergence of anxiety. You are not adding to it with thoughts about why you should or shouldn't be anxious or how to get rid of it. You just make a note of it. When anger, irritation, worry, fear, happiness, sexual urges, hunger, pain, planning your day, or wanting to burn your calculus text arise, call it by its name or label it to note it has entered your consciousness. Recognize whatever comes to mind by giving it a name, and return to your breath.

Element 3: State of Mind

Now that you've been introduced to the rudiments of how to sit and breathe, you can begin your meditation program. Keep in mind that the only two rules are: (1) begin, and (2) continue. Also, commit yourself to follow the general process of meditation, mindfulness, or Right Effort. This includes: (1) monitoring, staying alert, or paying attention; (2) recognizing when your mind wanders; (3) observing and letting be or witnessing and letting go of thoughts, feelings, and sensations that take you out of the moment; and (4) gently returning to the present moment.

Try to meditate everyday no matter how you feel. When you're happy, meditate. When you're sad, meditate. When you're exhausted from studying, meditate. When you discover Lama Phodopus Sungorus, the hamster who is your spiritual guide, is a fraud, meditate. But if you miss meditation, don't dwell on it. Don't beat yourself up. There's always the next time.

Ending (and Desire to End) Meditation: A Special Time

The topic of time often comes to mind during meditation in a variety of ways. Sometimes estimating when the meditation session will end takes our awareness from our breath. At other times, a strong desire for the sitting period to end is an impediment to staying in the moment.

Dealing with questions of how much time has gone by and how much more there is to go requires that you use the general practice of mindfulness to bring your mind back to the present moment.

Attitude of Mind or Focus of Meditation

The practice is to stay aware of what you are doing or simply focusing on the process of breathing in and breathing out. It's a practice you probably won't find easy, but each time you do it, you benefit.

To sit and lull yourself into a trance is not the purpose of meditation. To strive for some special experience is not the purpose of meditation. The right mental attitude for meditation is an alert yet relaxed mind. The aim of meditation is not an inactive or an overactive mind. Your intention in meditation is to allow your naturally attentive, open, and observant mind to emerge in the present moment.

The objective of meditation is to rest your attention on the object of meditation such as the breath. However, meditation should not be framed as forced concentration or a "keep your mind on the object or primary focus of meditation or burn in the fires of hell" approach.

Intention and Determination

Learning about how our mind operates is one of the purposes of meditation. By intentionally observing, not analyzing, how our mind works during meditation, we come to see where our mind wanders and how we get stuck in irrelevant thoughts and feelings. In meditation practice, we learn the value of simply letting thoughts, emotions, and sensations dissipate on their own. The process of meditation and practice of Right Effort in all areas of life will help us to live a more effective and satisfying life.

Intention and commitment are essential to establishing the consistent operation of Right Effort in your life. The more that you apply Right Effort with the appropriate intent and attitude, the better you get at it.

Just before you begin a period of meditation (or anything else), you may find it helpful to make a commitment to accept whatever arises during the meditation period and return time after time to resting in the breath.

You place your trust in the process. Meditation is the practice of "learning to stay." It is a commitment to remain present with whatever arises while you sit, and it's a pact to return to the present whenever you waver.[33]

The Place of Goals in Meditation

As we presented in the first few pages of this book, there are many desirable effects of meditation, for example, reduced anxiety, increased mental acuity, and even positive changes in brain structure and functioning. Meditation can contribute to more effective learning, which is not only important while you are in school but also throughout your life. Given that one of your goals in practicing meditation may be to enjoy its beneficial results, it may not strike you as sensible that you should let go of goals while meditating. It seems paradoxical that disregarding the positive results of meditation while meditating is necessary for realizing the benefits of meditation.

---

33   Chodron, 2001

Insight Meditation teacher Dr. Larry Rosenberg puts it this way, "This is the deepest paradox in all of meditation: we want to get somewhere – we wouldn't have taken up the practice if we didn't – but the way to get there is just to be fully here. The way to get from point A to point B is really to be at point A."[34]

The importance of opening to the present moment cannot be emphasized enough. The point of all meditation practices is to develop your ability to stay fully in touch with whatever is the present reality and letting be what is not in the present, including goals and potential benefits. If you do this, results naturally follow.

Meditation and Thinking

Meditation is "not thinking." Meditation is also "not not thinking." As noted before, committing yourself to "not think" is a great way to promote thought. Meditation is sometimes characterized as "non-thinking."

There is nothing wrong with thinking. There is plenty to recommend it. Thinking is natural for humans. Our ability to think has been a blessing, it accounts for the success of our species. The evolution of our brains and minds to where we are capable of rational thought has resulted in tremendous advantages for humankind.

Although the ability to think at the rational level is of great benefit, and everyone should develop the ability to think, most of the thinking done by people is not at the rational or modern level. As noted earlier, research shows that most of us to do not think at the rational level most of the time. Often wayward thoughts below the rational level get in the way of productive and creative thinking. This is

---

34   Rosenberg, 1998, p. 33

where meditation or the practice of attention, mindfulness, or non-thinking can help. It improves our thinking.

Here is how it works. Much of our thinking is in the pre-rational state. Most of the thinking that we do is also discursive thinking, which is "…to move from topic to topic without order."[35] In this sense, it is the opposite of what we generally think of as analytical thinking, creative flow, and focus.

Another characteristic of our typical state of mind is incessant chatter. Our minds are always commenting on something. We like this and we don't like that. Many meditation instructors refer to this typical or ordinary state of mind as "monkey mind." It's not meant to be a compliment.

Our usual state of mind is to follow whatever pops up. Most of this thought is unproductive in the sense that it doesn't help us to solve problems at the rational level. There is nothing wrong with discursive thought as long as we only give it the attention it deserves. When we get stuck in discursive thinking and get dragged away from what we are supposed to be doing or intend to do in the present moment, it becomes a problem. When a chattering mind, drifting mind, or scattered mind gets in the way of doing what needs to be done and keeps us off track, it is an impediment to effective performance and attaining our goals.

Meditation teaches us to deal with discursive and intrusive thoughts. We learn to keep returning to our object of meditation. In the same way, when we apply these lessons from meditation to learning, it helps us to keep our focus on what we are thinking about and the way we should be thinking about it.

---

35   Merriam-Webster's, 1998, p. 332

Chapter 9

Where We've Been, Where We're Going, and Where We Didn't Go

*P*art One* of this book introduced you to its central theme: paying attention. It's an ability we all think is important. Indeed, it would be hard to find a student, professor, or anyone else who doesn't think the capacity to pay attention is essential for doing just about anything well. It would be equally difficult to find a sizeable number of people in higher education who have been taught and regularly practice an effective method for paying attention.

Plenty of people in our lives have told us to pay attention. They just never gave us detailed instructions on how to do it. Nonetheless, most of us manage to find an approach to paying attention. Unfortunately, the most common approach adopted is relatively ineffective.

The combat model is the most common method of paying attention. When this aggressive approach is applied to schoolwork, learning becomes a fight with our books as the enemy (FWB). An alternative view of learning is a dance with our books as our partners (DWB).

Dancing With Your Books reflects Right Effort in Buddha's program for mind development. It's a task- or process-centered approach in which attention to the activity of the moment is emphasized. Goals and objectives are of great importance because they shape what we do in the present and give direction for the future. However, any attention we allocate to the future or past while we are involved in an activity in the present takes away from the activity of the moment.

The other aspect of Buddha's program incorporated into the DWB approach is Right Meditation. As we've seen, Right Meditation is the application of Right Effort to the task of just sitting and breathing. It's also a way to develop Right Effort. Simply by observing our own thoughts, feelings, and sensations without judgment, we learn about the operation of our own minds. We discover the kind of receptive attention and responsiveness that is the opposite of forced concentration and reactivity.

In the next part of the book, we'll present another perspective on Right Effort drawn from Robert Pirsig's *Zen and the Art of Motorcycle Maintenance.*[36] The focus will be on some specific problems that can diminish Right Effort and how to deal with them.

---

36   Pirsig, 1974

Part II

Maintaining Quality and Enthusiasm

Chapter 10

Gumption

A great deal of what we have discussed in this book is also explored using the examples of riding and repairing motorcycles in Robert Pirsig's classic, *Zen and the Art of Motorcycle Maintenance: An Inquiry Into Values.* Millions of copies of Pirsig's book have been sold since the mid-seventies, and he attributes much of its success to the influence of college professors recommending the book to their students.

Just like the dance and dancer are one in the act of dancing, Pirsig's view is that there is no separation between person and task while working on a motorcycle. This absorption in the task produces what Pirsig calls Quality, and he refers to the attitude that promotes Quality as gumption.

Gumption is Pirsig's term for a down home version of Right Effort. It means that you are aware of reality and

embrace it. You do what needs to be done without sniv-
eling, self-pity, or self-indulgence. You don't waste your
time wishing things were different. When you have gumption, you meet the world on its terms in all its complexity
and beauty in each moment.

When you approach a task with gumption, it is done
with enthusiasm and an open, quiet mind. There is no rush.
Whatever the task, you know you have to stick with it until
it's done, and you also know that the doing is more important than what gets done. There is always more to be done.
It is how you do it in the moment that really counts.

Chapter 11

Gumption Traps

Gumption traps are obstacles to approaching tasks with Right Effort. They are impediments to adopting the process-centered perspective and realizing intrinsic satisfaction. The most general advice that can be offered on handling gumption traps is that as soon as you realize one has grabbed you, consider it a sign that you are being unmindful or mindless. You should gently return to a mindful approach by doing whatever you're supposed to be doing in the present moment.

The gumption trap can be seen as a call to mindfulness and an opportunity to practice. Through practice, you transform the situation from one in which you were losing gumption into one in which your gumption is restored or even increased.

Throughout the discussion of gumption traps, many techniques will be suggested for gumption promotion and restoration. You can't possibly practice them all or even a handful during any one time period. Don't even think about trying.

The best way is to select the gumption trap that gives you the most difficulty. Pick what you consider the best technique for dealing with it, and implement it into your approach to learning and any other areas of your life. You will discover, as we have, that one of the biggest impediments to practicing the technique you select is to remember to do it. Use any method to remember that you think will help. Put a post-it note on your bathroom mirror; write the name of the technique on your hand; set it as the background on your phone; get the technique tattooed on your forearm, if you need to, or even better, your best friend's forehead. Just do something to help you to remember.

Chapter 12

Gumption Trap I: Ego

We already know that self-centeredness can take us out of the moment and make the experience of flow or joyful doing impossible. This is what we mean by ego. It is excessive and damaging focus on self that interferes with being fully present. An important point we want to stress is that it is a misunderstanding to think that having an ego is something bad. We can't function well in this world without a healthy ego. The ego gumption trap represents a dysfunctional or unhealthy ego. Part of our practice is to get our ego functioning as well as possible.

Monster Ego

We all know people who have monster egos. These are people who think the sun shines only on them; others were placed on earth to admire them; and life is a movie in which they have the starring role and everyone else is the supporting cast. In their view, what they say and do matters to everyone, and their parents are very lucky to be related to them.

The monster ego is too full of himself to be deeply involved in anything he is doing. If what life brings to be done in the moment does not enhance the ego by advertising his worth to the world, then he thinks that it is not worth doing. The task itself doesn't matter much to the monster ego. What matters is that it is he who is doing the task. The task is only of significance because it has implications for his aggrandizement.

Although students are adequately represented in the ranks of monster egos, these gargantuan egos are more often found in academia in the form of rigid and defensive professors who launch venomous attacks on anyone who questions their cherished position on an issue. For such professors, a display of open-mindedness or tolerance for opposing views is not a chink in their armor; it's a gaping hole of vulnerability.

The man with an immense ego, let's call him Professor M. Ego, thinks his ideas must be defended at all costs. This may be especially difficult in the face of the most powerful adversary, valid contradictory evidence. Here, there are a number of effective strategies available to Professor Ego. One of the most common is to disregard or categorically dismiss any evidence that refutes his argument. If people do not agree with him, they are simply wrong. It is being right that is so important to Professor M. Ego. The threat of being wrong is so powerful that he closes his mind to any information that could potentially invalidate his claims. This obviously has a negative influence on his teaching, research, and his own learning.

Professor Ego's focus on being seen as right and enhancing his status clearly works against him. Research demonstrates that academics primarily concerned with status and advancing their careers produce lower quality work than those who concentrate mainly on their work because they find it intrinsically satisfying. Those with monster egos are considerably more *extrinsically* than *intrinsically* motivated. This negatively affects the quality of their performance both in their research and teaching as well as their level of satisfaction with their work.[37]

Student Monster Egos

As noted above, monster egos seem to be less common among students. Perhaps they're less prevalent because traditionally aged students haven't had enough time to develop fully into monster egos. Monster egos do, however, exist among students, and they can take several forms. One particularly offensive kind is arrogance. Here we have the Mr. and Ms. Know-It-Alls of the campus. Their view is that there is really nothing they can be taught about a subject, and they are enrolled in a particular course or program only because it is a requirement to obtain a needed credential. The attitude that there is nothing of value to be learned just about guarantees that they will learn nothing. When egos are puffed up to this size, thoughts of self-importance take up all available mental space. There is no room for learning.

Consider the number of students who begin college or select a particular major solely for instrumental reasons. Their central purpose, for example, may be to improve their marketability. This is not a bad idea. Higher education does

---

37   Johnson, Johnson, and Smith, 1991

increase the value of graduates on the employment market. But college has more to offer than economic value. To insist that the only purpose of higher education is to increase your economic potential limits the benefits of education for you. Paradoxically, it can even diminish attaining the practical and economic goals of attending college.

To some extent, exclusive focus on extrinsic results or the practical benefits of college can be considered a form of conceit. This is the case with a guy named Student M. Ego. His focus only on the instrumental is a manifestation of Student M. Ego's sense of superiority. His claim is that he knows the true value of education and it's unreasonable to suggest he adopt a broader view. If Student M. Ego determines that the content of a course does not have a direct and obvious connection to enhancing his attractiveness to potential employers, the course is considered valueless.

Obtaining a college degree for instrumental reasons or extrinsic rewards is neither uncommon nor unreasonable. Most of us go to college for these reasons. Instrumental reasons such as career, money, and security can become a problem, however, if you constantly focus on how a course will make you look in the eyes of someone else, e.g., potential employers.

There are two dangers here that Student M. Ego can encounter. First, he could be wrong about what will and will not improve his marketability. If nothing else, times change and so do employment requirements. The second hazard of this strictly instrumental approach to learning is that it limits Student Ego's chances of experiencing flow and enjoyment in learning in the present.

To experience anything in terms of only what it can do for you in an ulterior way precludes experiencing the joy of it. The good news is you can experience the pleasure of learning and get a good job when you graduate. They are not mutually exclusive, indeed, they are related.

Here's an example of how a course taken just for intrinsic reasons can later have huge instrumental value. As everyone knows, the late Steve Jobs, the former president of Apple, dropped out of college and became a popular exemplar of the unimportance of a college education. After he withdrew from college, however, Steve Jobs did not drop out of campus life, including taking college courses. He stayed around and took courses that he thought were interesting. He took a course in calligraphy because he was captured by the beauty of it. He never imagined that it would have instrumental value or a practical application. But it did. A decade later when he was developing the Macintosh computer, his knowledge of calligraphy was essential in designing some of the features of the Mac that distinguished it from other personal computers.[38]

Ego Monsters

We all know people who have ego monsters. These are people with fragile egos and low self-regard. They think the sun shines on everyone but them; others were placed on earth to make them look bad by comparison; life is a movie in which they can't even get a role as an extra; anything they say or do will only embarrass them; and their parents are humiliated to admit they are related to them.

Those with ego monsters are characterized by low self-worth, fear of failure, repressed anger, and feelings of inadequacy. They avoid tests and challenges, stick to the well-trodden path, and abhor all that is novel. Instead of accepting what life brings to be done in the moment, they

---

38   Jobs, June 14, 2005

withdraw or operate within a circumscribed life arena. This is a formula for avoiding anything challenging and complex, which is a necessary condition for growth and flow.

While attending school, the person who suffers from an ego monster, let's call him Student E. Monster, is convinced that he will fail any test he takes. During his academic career, there are at least several exams that he never takes because he is immobilized by pretest anxiety and fear of failure. Student E. Monster withdraws from at least one course a semester before he receives any evaluation from the professor because in his eyes his failure is a certainty. He has to enroll in the most demanding courses required for his degree in his last year because he could not face them until he absolutely had to take them.

E. Monster's friends and roommates are often sympathetic at the beginning of the semester. But soon, they find his incessant self criticism, his constant lack of confidence, and his defeatist attitude grating. When E. Monster does well on an exam or paper, he cannot bring himself to take credit for it. He attributes his success to luck, mistakes in grading, and/or divine intervention. When he does consistently well, he is convinced that he will be found out to be a fraud and publicly disgraced.

Common Ground

At first glance, E. Monster and M. Ego may appear to be completely different kinds of people. But this is not the case. Both suffer from the same malady: They are taken out of the moment by a preoccupation with self. Because of their self-focus, they are never immersed in the present doing what life brings to be done. They suffer from time-place dissonance, and this limits their chances of experiencing flow, quality, and intrinsic satisfaction. Thoughts of the consequences of their actions interfere with their performance and produce anxiety. In the case of M. Ego, anxiety is a call to action. E. Monster, on the other hand, is immobilized by it.

Several psychologists who have studied stress and anxiety point out that people who constantly engage in self-focus and self-assessment suffer from high anxiety. Over a quarter century ago, Norman Endler, a widely known expert on anxiety, reported "...anxiety is related to self-evaluation ... the highly anxious person is self-centered and focuses on self-evaluation and self-worry rather than on the situation or task."[39] The work of Mihaly Csikszentmilhalyi on flow or optimal experience also suggests that too much self-consciousness (not to be confused with consciousness or awareness) promotes anxiety and impedes flow.[40]

Ego Problems in Action

Ego concerns destroy gumption in that they keep your mind from learning what is before you, and they direct all your attention on you. You get stuck on you. You cannot possibly do a quality job or work enthusiastically under these circumstances. You can't get close enough to what you are supposed to learn because you are in the way. When your ego gets too big, you become immobile and inflexible. If there isn't any room for anything other than your ego, how do you expect to learn anything? It's like cramming your room so full of pictures of yourself that you don't have any room for the books, materials, and equipment you need for learning.

---

39   Endler,1980, p. 263

40   Csikszentmilhalyi, 1990

Learning with Right Effort or doing a quality job on any task requires humility. You must be open and accepting. If you have an ego the size of Montana, you won't develop these characteristics.

If your ego is so damaged that you are convinced that whatever you try to do will only advertise your incompetence to the world, it's a form of self-focus. Excessive thoughts of self are getting in your way. You constantly question your ability, and you always come up short.

Most of us do not suffer from ego problems of the magnitude of M. Ego and E. Monster. However, for all of us, our ability to perform to our full potential is compromised to some extent by ego concerns or self-absorption. The technique described in the next section is a method to become less self-focused and more in touch with whatever you're doing in a particular moment. It's a way to keep the ego in check.

"I" Drop for Diminishing Ego and Enhancing Gumption

Letting "I" go from your thoughts is an exercise you can practice to let the ego find where it belongs. The idea is that "I" gets between you and where you are so you become disconnected. You are separated from rather than merged in the present. Letting "I" drop gives you a chance to become more involved and interested in what you are doing, and more in touch with your surroundings.

Think small when you start. Letting go of "I" for even a short time is difficult. Start with a few minutes each day at the same time if possible. Each time you start thinking of yourself or each time "I" enters your consciousness, just label it an "I thought" and refocus your attention on what you are doing in the present moment. This way you nip "I" in the bud before it fully blooms. If you let "I" thoughts grow unchecked, they take over the whole garden, and there will be no room for anything else to grow.

A good way to start the "I" Drop practice is to apply it to a routine daily activity, e.g., showering or dish washing. You can also practice by trying to take your daily commute to school or work each day without "I." You don't have to kick "I" out of the car or off the bus. Just let him be, and he'll leave of his own accord. Any positive or negative attention to him keeps him around. He doesn't care what you think of him as long as you think of him.

Use the standard technique. First, recognize that you are thinking of "I" instead of driving or riding. This reduces the chance of "I" connecting with a bunch of other "I" thoughts" and turning into a full-blown "I" episode. Second, let "I" be. And third, return your full attention to what you are doing, that is, driving or riding or just breathing.

The first thing you'll experience when you start to deal with "I" is how difficult it is. You will notice that you think about yourself almost constantly, and soon after you recognize and let go of one "I" thought another pops, creeps, crashes, sneaks, cruises, struts, darts, worms, weasels, breaks, or bursts into consciousness. You'll see how clever "I" is. "I" knows that if he can convince you that the way to forget "I" is to actively not think of "I" then he has you. To not think of "I" is to think of "I." He also knows that when it is so hard to forget "I," you are susceptible to the following argument: If thoughts of "I" are unimportant or even harmful sometimes, then why does it seem so natural for you to constantly think about "I"?

By practicing the "I" Drop and focusing on what you are doing or where you are, you'll notice subtle changes. As you get better at your practice of paying attention to your walk to school, for example, instead of thoughts of "I," you'll start to notice all that you've been missing. You'll see trees and buildings on your daily route that you never knew existed, you'll notice leaves floating in puddles, the way babies straddle their mother's hip, a spider's web, the smell of autumn air, the human bustle of the morning rush. You'll begin to feel present and in touch with your surroundings. You'll realize that you are where you are supposed to be, which, of course, is where you are. Sometimes you'll ponder where "I" went. You'll chuckle and wonder how you could have thought that you couldn't live without "I." Then you'll become aware that "I" is still there, but he's finally in the right place where he becomes just I. The self hasn't disappeared. It's changed. It melds with whatever you are doing or wherever you are. There is no separation.

13

Gumption Trap 2: Value and Conceptual Rigidity

Value rigidity and its cousin, conceptual rigidity, occur when your opinion and perspective preclude you from seeing things in a new light or appreciating something new. You are incapable of seeing the world or some aspect of the world from any perspective other than yours. You reject anything that doesn't fit in with your view. If you are value-rigid or in a conceptual bind, you have trouble seeing certain facts and relationships. The patterns are there, but you can't see them through your current lens.

Most of us are limited by our commitment to the values and views of our cultural, social, political, and/or economic group. Those of us who are severely value or concept-rigid consider our way of seeing things as the only way. When we become too attached or identified with a certain view of the world, it can limit our creativity and impede our ability to solve problems.

Value and conceptual rigidity are the products of a closed mind. They are the antithesis of the receptive and open mind fostered by meditation called "beginner's mind" by Shunryu Suzuki in his classic book, *Zen Mind, Beginner's Mind*.[41] With beginner's mind, you enter a situation or approach a task without rigidly held preconceptions. You're ready for anything because you're open to everything. Your mind is supple and alert. If, on the other hand, your mind is value-rigid or concept- or frame-rigid, your approach is tense and brittle.

When you possess unyielding values and/or ways of framing or looking at things, your mind is the equivalent of your hand being closed in a fist. You can't pick up anything with a fist, it is impossible to grasp anything. About all you can do with your hand in a fist is to use it as a weapon. As with the hand, in order to grasp something, the mind must be open. You can't understand or learn with a closed mind. You can't pick up new ideas.

A characteristic associated with value rigidity is a tendency to assault people with your ideas about the way things are or should be or berate them for not accepting your views. Of course, there's none of that in this book, and, in the words of the late Lama Phodopus Sungourus," we'll beat the crap out of anyone who says there is."

---

41   Suzuki, 1970

The Value Rigid Monkey

In *Zen and The Art of Motorcycle Maintenance*, Pirsig presents the south Indian monkey trap as an illustration of value rigidity. The trap consists of a small box with a hole that is big enough for the monkey's opened hand to fit through, but is too small for his clenched fist to be pulled out. The trap is baited with rice, a banana, risotto with mussels and roasted garlic, or any other food a monkey would find appealing, which is just about anything. The trap is then fastened to a tree or stake. The monkey has no difficulty getting his hand into the trap. But once he grabs the food and forms a fist, he cannot get his hand out.

The obvious solution is to let go of the food and slip out of the trap. The monkey, however, so values the food that he doesn't let go. He cannot reassess the value of the food in light of his unexpected predicament. He desires the food at all costs, even his freedom. He keeps a tight fist around the food even as his captors approach.

Conceptual and Value Rigidity in Approaching Higher Education

One way value and conceptual rigidity can interfere with learning is when students prejudge a course or a professor. Required courses such as research methods and statistics in social science programs are often unpopular. The courses and some of those who teach them acquire horrible reputations. A substantial number of students enter these courses convinced that they are designed to produce a new dimension of pain. They assume that the content of such courses will be next to useless in the "real world." Given the choice between taking the course and a root canal, some students would have a hard time deciding.

It comes as no surprise that many students find these courses a torment. The problem generally is not the level of difficulty of the material. It really isn't that demanding. The problem is related to restricted values and concepts. Because many students refuse to let go of the notion that the courses are worthless and difficult, they don't even give the courses a chance.

The narrow-mindedness reflected in conceptual binds and value rigidity generally impedes learning. One area where these binds are especially troublesome is problem solving. Here, they limit the number and range of alternative solutions you can recognize or consider.

Conceptual Binds in Business and Industry

Donald Schon provides an example of the importance of a conceptual bind in his classic book, *Displacement of Concepts*.[42] He describes a sandal manufacturing firm that hired him to develop ways to deal with the problem of declining sales and revenue.

His first question when he arrived at the failing firm was to ask the executives what business they thought they were in. The company executives were put off by the question, and emphatically pointed out that it was obvious they were in the sandal business, a family business that had been in operation for many years. They told Donald Schon that it was categorically evident that they were exclusively in the business of sandals by a number of obvious indicators anyone could see: the sandal shaped sign on their building, the sandal shaped chair he was sitting in, the sandal shaped conference table at which he was sitting, the sandal lapel pins they were wearing, and the complementary water buffalo sandals he was given. The

42   Schon, 1963

name of the business, Sandal and Sons, should have been the most obvious tipoff. They took off their sandals and were about to give Schon a nasty sandal bashing, when he asked if they would humor him for a couple of minutes. Birkenstock Sandal, the youngest son, started the clock.

Schon suggested that their view of their business was their whole problem. They had too narrowly framed the business they were in. They were in a conceptual bind that limited the solutions to their problem. They had to take a broader view. They were so attached to the view of their firm as producing sandals that it blinded them to other options. Alternatives to making and marketing sandals were there, but they were so invested in seeing themselves in the sandal business, they saw only sandal solutions.

Donald Schon recommended that if they more broadly considered themselves as in the leisure footwear business, it would change just about everything, including the kind of business data they were analyzing. They would not only look at their sandal sales data, but they would also examine sandal sales as a component of the leisure footwear market. If they did this, they would see that at that time sandals were declining as a share of the leisure footwear market while other kinds of leisure and recreational footwear were increasing in popularity. It was the beginning of the trend in running shoes, boating shoes, and hiking boots for casual and recreational wear. In order to produce and market the increasingly popular new kinds of leisure footwear, the company could use their existing machinery, labor, sales forces, and distribution channels. The only major change they had to make was a change in frame, perspective, or the way they looked at the business they were in. They had to see themselves as out of the sandal business and in the leisure footwear business. They needed to break their conceptual bind and adopt a broader view.

Chapter 14

Gumption Trap 3: Anxiety

Anxiety is a common gumption trap that research indicates is a major source of poor academic performance. A review of over 100 research studies of academic performance and anxiety involving more than 30,000 students shows that academic performance decreases as anxiety increases.[43] Anxiety, like ego, drains gumption. Nervousness or worry about performance and its consequences gets in the way of performing well. You are so worried about how well you are going to do and how you will look in the eyes of others that it can take your attention away from what you're doing.

Of course, as you know by now, one way to deal with anxiety and to restore gumption is to keep your attention on the task itself. Just study when you study; focus on the exam while taking it. Don't worry about how stupid you're

---

43   Seipp study as cited in Goleman, 1995

going to look if you can't learn the material or worry you will fail while you are taking a test. You can't focus on what you're studying or the questions you're answering if you're busy dreading the consequences.

How do you keep your attention on the task itself? Simply practice. Use the same techniques that you use in meditation and any mindfulness practices. When thoughts about embarrassment and other consequences of poor performance enter your mind, just recognize them for what they are, let them be, and return to your work. Don't criticize yourself for having intrusive thoughts. Be confident that the thoughts will pass if you don't try to indulge them or suppress them.

There are three areas of your educational experience where anxiety can be especially troublesome: asking professors or instructors questions, presentations, and taking tests.

Asking Questions

Reluctance to ask questions publicly is often linked to fear of looking stupid. You are convinced that everyone else knows the answer to the question you are about to ask, and if you ask the question, you may be nominated for the bonehead of the decade award, which is given every eleven years. So you sit silently and avoid disclosing your secret. You feel better knowing that no one will ever know you're a closet moron. Of course, when the question you should have asked in class appears on the exam, it might be pretty evident to your professor that you should have been asking questions.

The practice of not asking questions that should be asked in lectures, seminars, and even informal study groups destroys gumption. Your enthusiasm for learning is dampened by preoccupation with yourself and how you'll look in front of your instructors and your peers. If you have honestly tried to learn the material, and if you want clarification or elaboration, ask questions. Even if you feel that you can't articulate a question very well, ask anyway. Most professors who have been teaching for a few years become pretty good at deciphering what you mean. Sometimes the professor or a fellow student merely restating your question is all that is needed for understanding.

Try asking a few questions without considering how you look or despite how you think you look. Think of it as an exercise in building gumption. You will see how truly liberating it really is.

No doubt you do not consider this method proposed for reducing the anxiety of asking questions difficult to grasp. As with most things, the conceptual understanding part is pretty easy. Clearly, putting it into practice is the hard part. Opening your mouth and squeaking out the question is where many of us get stuck. The question becomes "How can these guys seriously recommend we face this situation without a doppelganger or stunt double?" The answer is "We can't. We can't for you and we can't for us."

The best we can do is to try to convince you that although we joke around about this stuff, we're not really joking around. We realize how difficult it is for many of us to ask a serious and worthwhile question in class. We know this from our personal experience and watching others. All we can suggest is that you try and keep trying. We realize that to recommend something like this is a platitude among platitudes. But sometimes a cliché is as good as it gets.

Asking questions in class is not a burden that should be entirely borne by individual students. Instructors must provide a classroom environment in which students want to ask questions. As part of an appropriate setting for asking questions, professors must let students know that, like all professors, they don't know everything, but that they are willing to find out or help students to find out.

Good professors want students to ask questions. They may indicate areas where they may not have been clear, and it may highlight points that they should have addressed but missed.

Students are also responsible for promoting a learning environment in which other students feel comfortable asking questions. Actions like talking to others while someone is asking a question, known as cross-talking, can interfere. Cross-talking, which is obviously disrespectful, should be avoided not only when someone is asking a question but also whenever someone, either the professor or a student, has the floor, i.e., they are addressing the class.

Expressing Opinions and Perspectives

Just because everyone has an opinion, it does not mean that all opinions are of equal value. While it may be true that everyone is entitled to an opinion, there are various validity criteria by which we judge the value of opinions, arguments, statements, and observations. The criteria include logic, plausibility, and research or empirical support. Some opinions meet the criteria better than others. We suggest that you consider validity standards or the soundness of your opinions, arguments, and/or observations before you express them. Remember: Just because you've thought of something doesn't mean that it's true.

There are situations when you won't examine your opinions, views, and/or conclusions by the standards of soundness. For example, if you're told to just throw out ideas spontaneously for a classroom discussion. Another time is when you are convinced that your perspective should be expressed because you feel strongly that it's worthwhile. In this situation, be sure to mention that personal intuition is the basis of your view. What's most important is that you take a chance and put opinions, judgments, and observations out there in order to learn.

The Proper View of Argument or Debate

Many of us have a misconception of argument or debate. The purpose is not to browbeat opponents into submission. According to Professor David Zarefsky, "Far from the stereotypes of contentiousness or quarrelsomeness, argumentation...is concerned with communication that seeks to persuade others through reasoned judgment."[44] Argumentation can be seen as a form of decision making in which those involved state their positions along with supporting evidence to an audience that decides which position is most reasonable.

In an argument or debate, the parties proposing positions or claims agree on certain rules or standards of evidence and all participants in the argument accept the risk of being wrong. It's important for participants in an argument to be aware that they don't necessarily have it right, and they can learn from their fellow participants.

Participants in an argument agree to act as "critical listeners" for others involved. This is part of the process to determine the comparative strength of positions or

---

44   Zarefsky, 2005, p. 1

claims. The exchange of positions on issues, evidence supporting claims, and assessments derived from critical listening often results in participants learning, and in some cases, even adopting an entirely new point of view on an issue. Of course, the possibility of our changing our view in response to an argument by another requires openness on our part. Openness is a personal quality that can be developed through the practice of mindfulness. Clearly, people like Professor M. Ego are not worthy participants for a proper debate or argument.

Presentations

A proper classroom environment is not only important for promoting questions and expressing a variety of views, but it is also important when students are making presentations, which is another source of anxiety. Fear of public speaking is common, and most of us experience at least mild anxiety when we have to talk in front of a group. If we consider our audience hostile, rather than civil, our anxiety may amplify and combine with counter-hostility.

The source of anxiety when preparing for a presentation and presenting is, of course, a focus on results, especially on how we will look or what the audience will think of our performance. One way to reduce anxiety is to be prepared. Obviously, if you prepare well, it increases the chances that you'll present well and portray the image of a competent and knowledgeable speaker. So adequate preparation should decrease your concern with how you will look.

Try to stay in the moment when preparing and presenting by following the prescriptions for Right Effort. Focus on what you are doing not on yourself. When thoughts other than the material you are presenting come to mind, note them, and let them be. If you're nervous about your presentation, don't fight it. Just observe it. As you already know, attempting not to be nervous or trying to push it out of your consciousness won't do you much good.

Here are a couple of practical tips that have been offered by some habitually nervous public speakers. One is to pick a sympathetic person in the audience and focus on him or her. You can usually find a person with a kind face in the audience who seems to be encouraging you to speak. Pretend you are presenting only to them. Let your eyes scan the entire the audience once in a while so you appear to be addressing everyone. But don't focus the delivery of your presentation on anyone except your sympathetic listener.

A second approach is to picture everyone in your audience as a baby. No one is afraid of a bunch of babies, unless, of course, they are crying or need to be changed. Infants aren't going to understand you anyway so there's no need to be anxious about what you have to say.

Exams

Obviously, tests are another major cause of anxiety among students. For many, they are the most serious cause. Heart pounding, hands sweating, nerves racing out of control, you pick up your pen or place your fingers on the keyboard to answer the first question but nothing happens. You sit there in a state of shock, while the test goes on. Sound familiar? It does to us and many other victims of test anxiety, a kind of performance anxiety that ranges from mild tension to complete immobilization.

One of the best ways to deal with test anxiety is to prepare well for the examination and have confidence in your preparation. Start studying early for the test, and study with Right Effort. Get ready for the test so you enter without a doubt in your mind that you did everything you could to adequately prepare. Know there is nothing more you could have done. All that remains is to take the test with Right Effort and gumption. Become fully absorbed in the test. If all the while you are taking the test you are thinking that you should have studied more or better or you're wishing the test was over, you are not in touch with what you are doing. As you do in meditation and other practices, keep bringing your mind back to what you are supposed to be doing, i.e., just testing.

If during the exam or while studying for the exam you feel a sudden surge of anxiety or you feel your mind racing out of control, try the following exercise. Take a deep breath through your nose using your diaphragm, and fill your lungs to their full capacity. As you feel the air draw in, think of it as a fresh, calming stream coming into your body. As you expel air through your nose, think of it as the anxiety leaving your body. Repeat the exercise three times. If you don't have time for three repetitions, one breath is sufficient.

The exercise just described is known as "cleansing breath." A variation is described in Bo Lozoff's *We're All Doing Time,* which is a book of advice and practices for prison inmates.[45] If this technique can help prisoners deal with the fear, anxiety, and frustration of confinement in a maximum-security prison, it should do wonders for test anxiety.

Another way to reduce test anxiety and enhance performance is to write about your worries before the test. There is experimental evidence in studies done at the University of Chicago that supports this technique. Students who

45   Lozoff, 1989

were given the opportunity to write about their worries shortly before an exam reduced their anxiety and scored higher than those who were not given the chance to write. The technique worked even with highly anxious students.

Professor Sian Bellock, the senior investigator on the study, thinks the results of the study can be generalized to a variety of situations. "... [W]e think this type of writing will help people perform their best in variety of pressure-filled situations – whether it is a big presentation to a client, a speech to an audience or even a job interview."[46]

---

46   University of Chicago News Office, January 13, 2011

Chapter 15

Gumption Trap 4: Boredom

The fourth internal gumption trap is boredom, which is characterized by a lack of interest. The two ingredients of interest are (1) a sufficiently challenging task that is given meaning by being part of an important goal, and (2) a person capable of being interested. The lack of these elements is the source of boredom.

Once an activity is part of the larger goal, it has more value. In serving the larger purpose, which has meaning for you, it should be more interesting. If it's interesting and valuable, it deserves your attention. Here's a story that illustrates a way to broadly frame just about any activity.

Laying Bricks

Long ago and far away, there was a man taking a stroll. He came upon three brick masons. They were working about 100 feet apart on the foundation of a huge structure. The man was curious. He stopped by the first worker and asked him what he was doing. The bricklayer shot the man a look of contempt and replied, "What the (expletive deleted) does it look like I'm doing? I'm laying (expletive deleted) bricks."

The man moved down the line and asked the second bricklayer the same question. He cheerfully responded, "I'm building a wall."

When the man asked the third brick mason the question, he turned his full attention toward the man. His face was serene and his eyes twinkled with enthusiasm as he responded, "I'm building a cathedral."[47]

It is evident that the meaning of the work for the third man was more significant than to the other two brick masons. Physically or in a material sense, i.e., in terms of the external or exterior dimension of the job, the men were doing exactly the same work, and we can assume they were earning the same pay for what they were doing. The only factor that made the experience different for the men was the way they saw it, which is the interior or internal dimension of the job or the way the mind views it. The first two men had relatively narrow views of what they were doing. Compared to our man who saw his job as building a cathedral, the other two workers appear to lead impoverished work lives. Laying bricks and building walls are pretty insignificant work compared to building a cathedral. Because he saw his work as so important, we

---

47   Based on Stevens et al., 1984

can assume that the third brick mason took more interest and care in what he was doing than did the other two. We can also assume that he experienced more intrinsic satisfaction and less boredom.

This story has implications for all kinds of work, including schoolwork. You can interpret an activity in a narrow sense, and see your work in a particular moment as reading a chapter or completing a problem set, which is the equivalent of laying bricks. Or you can see anything you are doing for school as getting an education, which is the equivalent of building a cathedral. The broader view, i.e., getting an education or building a cathedral, makes the activity more meaningful and more worthy of your complete attention. At an even broader level, everything you do, no matter how mundane, is part of living your life, your "real life." The only life you have is the one you are living in this very moment. You have a cathedral right in front of you in this moment. You just have to recognize it, and get to work.

Building in Breaks

Sometimes you should take a break when you find yourself bored or you should systematically build breaks into your work schedule. Return to the task after you have had a short period of meditation or sleep, a cup of coffee, or a bit of entertainment. Keep in mind, however, that boredom that doesn't respond to a break can be a symptom of chronic boredom – a serious gumption problem.

Chronic boredom means it is time for a Right Effort check. You may have let yourself slip into the habit of just going through the motions. You're no longer fully involved, and you let thoughts of other times and places rescue you from what you now see as drudgery. It is time to get back on track. Take some time to meditate. Then reaffirm your commitment to your goal of getting an education and working with Right Effort on each task related to your goal. Work for short periods of time, taking breaks between them, until your gumption reservoir refills. Sometimes, even when your gumption is at full power, you should count a few breaths between chapters or assignments as a way to maintain your gumption.

Occasionally, you should schedule a "big break"–a day or even an entire weekend or longer between semesters. Keep in mind, however, that moderation is the key to returning refreshed from the "big break." If your break becomes a "lost weekend," it will be enervating instead of restorative. In other words, don't act like a Shaltoonian.

Shaltoon

Those of you who are familiar with Kilgore Trout's epic science fiction saga, *Venus on the Halfshell,* will recall that the Space Wanderer, Simon Wagstaff, an Earthman who travels through the universe with an atomic-powered banjo, a female robot, an owl, and a dog, spends a short time on Shaltoon, a planet on which there is ancestor rotation.[48]

Each Shaltoonian is made up of cells that contain the memories of all of his or her ancestors. Once a Shaltoonian reaches puberty, his or her body is taken over by one of these ancestors each day of the week, except one. Shaltoonian years are twice as long as earth years and the life expectancy of a Shaltoonian is two thousand years. This means that the more dominant ancestors will appear at least once during a Shaltoonian's lifetime.

---

48   Trout, 1974; Kilgore Trout was created by Kurt Vonnegut.

As a result of ancestor rotation, Shaltoon never advanced beyond a simple agricultural society. The reason that ancestor rotation and progress are incompatible is obvious if you've ever met a Shaltoonian. When an ancestor takes over the body, he is not about to spend his day working on labor-saving devices, plans to restructure the economy, or a philosophical treatise on the rights of the host body. Although the ancestor is expected to do some work to ensure that society continues, a large part of his day is spent in the frenzied fulfillment of carnal desires and other appetites. On most days, the planet of Shaltoon is a place of collective depravity, and very little work gets done.

Each ancestor, when given the opportunity, eats, drinks, and copulates with wild abandon. The majority of the population on any given day is rocking out in the fast lane. The order of the day, every day, is to consume compulsively at a frenetic pace. Life is an orgy; all of Shaltoon is a raucous party every day.

Sounds pretty good to some, but occasionally somebody has to suffer for the outrageous behavior of his predecessors. Consider the poor Shaltoonian who inhabits the body when it can no longer endure the magnitude of the effects of immoderation. The hangover of the stricken Shaltoonian is like a nuclear explosion in the head with nausea more powerful than a tsunami. On any given day, the excesses of their ancestors incapacitate a large proportion of Shaltoonians. As Kilgore Trout describes it, "Every once in a while, the body would collapse and be carried off to a hospital by drunken ambulance attendants and turned over to drunken nurses and doctors. The poor devil who had possession that day was too sick to do anything but lie in bed, groaning and cursing."[49] As everyone who has spent

---

49   Trout, 1974, p. 64

too much time in the fast lane will tell you, eventually it catches up with you and the after effects can be formidable.

The moral of the story is, of course, don't act like a Shaltoonian ancestor when you take your big break. You are the host body who has to return to your studies.

The Futility of Multitasking as a Solution to Boredom or Anything Else

Some consider multitasking an antidote to boredom and a way to increase productivity. For many people, multitasking is a way of life, and intentionally doing one thing at a time is a rare experience.

Today, multitasking is seen as an adaptation to the exponentially increasing rapid pace of life. In addition to being seen as a survival requirement, it's also considered a measure of competence and a source of status and pride.

The problem with multitasking is that it doesn't work that well, especially for anything novel or complex. Research evidence shows that it is not a very efficient and effective way to accomplish tasks. It decreases speed and performance and increases mistakes.[50] Obviously, when you are attempting to do a number of things at once, it limits the attention that you can devote to any one activity. The reality is that you typically don't actually perform more than one complex single mental task at a time. You just *think* of yourself as doing more than one thing at a time. Much of mental multitasking is an illusion. For the most part, you are engaging mental tasks in rapid succession, and you may be switching back and forth between them. For example, you are not actually reading, texting, and talking on the phone all at the same time. You're mind

50   Lohr, 2005; Wisdom 2.0, 2009

actually zips from task to task. You imperceptibly bounce back and forth.

If you read when you read, text when you text, and talk when you talk, it will take you less time to complete all the tasks than when you use a multitasking approach, and you will do a better job than with multitasking. When your mind rockets between tasks, you are constantly breaking your concentration. You are not focused on any one task long enough to do a good job.

We all multitask and it's unlikely that we are going to change in today's technological environment. But we should try to keep our multitasking to simple activities. This way the effects on our efficiency and effectiveness in task performance are minimal.

One of the important lessons learned from meditation and other mindfulness practices is the art of uni-tasking or mono-tasking. Meditation can be seen as the practice of doing one thing at a time with full attention. It takes time and effort to learn how to uni-task, but as we've seen in the presentation of mindfulness and Right Effort, it's well worth it. Once you learn to pay full attention to the activity of the moment, you can do it better in less time, and what you are doing becomes more interesting and satisfying.

Daydream and Fantasy

Many of us daydream and/or fantasize as a reaction to boredom. Frequently, we just let our minds meander when we are supposed to be paying attention to an assigned task. Although most of us don't consider it a form of multitasking, it can be seen as one. It's an attempt to accomplish the task of the moment while at the same time daydreaming as a way of handling the tedium associated with tasks. Obviously, it qualifies as an interruption from which you have to recover to get back on task.

Go ahead and daydream when your time is not otherwise occupied. However, when your daydreams arise while you are supposed to be listening to a lecture or reading a book, for instance, they destroy attention to the moment. Recognize these distractions from the work of the moment, and gently return to what you're supposed to be doing.

16

Gumption Trap 5:
Lack of Energy and Interest

The energy and interest trap is a relative of the boredom trap. Here, you wonder when you begin a task if you will have what it takes to make it through. Your concern is that sometime during the performance of the task your energy and interest will dissipate to the point where you're bored, tired, and frustrated. You're afraid that somewhere before the completion of the project your initial enthusiasm and resolve to do a quality job will be replaced by drudgery and exhaustion. What's the sense of even starting? Why not wait until some other time when you know you have the energy and interest to carry you through?

Lack of energy is a symptom of a lack of mindfulness. When multiple thoughts, including doubts about your energy and interest, are occupying your mind, it saps your energy from what you're doing. One effect of your meditation practice is that it helps you focus all your energy on one task.

Confidence

As just indicated, one problem that creates the energy and interest trap is a lack of confidence. You are unsure of your ability to sustain the level of vitality and intellectual stimulation needed to do the job. One solution is that when your confidence wanes, accept whatever shortcomings you perceive, surrender to the task, and get on with the job. Let go of those self-centered thoughts about what you can and can't do, and just do the best you can.

Don't make the mistake of checking with your feelings to see if you should begin a project or continue one. You should, of course, be aware of your feelings and observe them. But, this doesn't mean you should ask for their permission to start or continue by inquiring about your reserves of energy and motivation. It will take your attention away from the present and the task at hand. When such questions do arise, recognize them for what they are, and let them be. Don't even try to give a yes-or-no answer to starting or continuing what you should be doing. Simply move ahead. Take a step on the path shaped by your goals with all your doubts and concerns. Then, take the next step. And the next.

Universal Energy

You can build confidence in your store of energy by realizing that it is limitless. You have all the energy in the universe at your disposal. Techniques for tapping into the universal source of energy, known as *ki* in Japanese, are commonly taught in the Japanese martial arts. A similar concept, *drala*, is part of the Tibetan Shambhala tradition. In Hinduism, it is called *prana*, the "breath of life," which is linked to the power of all creation. One technique for tapping into the limitless source of energy is to visualize as you breathe in that you inhale the energy of the universe into your body and mind. Let its force surge through you so that you feel restored, refreshed, invigorated.

Imagine that you share in the infinite energy of the universe. Feel secure in knowing that universal energy is available to you. This should have a calming effect, which in turn makes more energy available to you. You won't waste energy by worrying about its availability when you are sure of a plentiful supply from an inexhaustible source.

Chapter 17

Gumption Trap 6: Impatience

You are most likely to fall into the impatience trap when you underestimate how long it will take you to complete a task. Unanticipated problems are common when working on just about anything, and unless you are prepared to deal with them, you can become frustrated and angry when you encounter them. These emotions can, of course, deplete your gumption and diminish the quality of your effort.

You should plan a modest amount of work, and give yourself plenty of time to do it. It is a mistake to think that you can write a research paper or complete a project in one day. Some impatience, frustration, and anxiety can be avoided if you break down the job or assignment into manageable parts, and you give yourself enough time to complete each part without rushing.

Of course, one sure way to get yourself into the impatience trap is to wait until the last minute by convincing yourself that you only work well under pressure. The strategy of postponing a task to maximize inspiration and motivation is almost certain to backfire. It creates a situation where you work frantically with all your attention on the outcome of meeting the deadline and you lose focus on the task itself. You get edgy and irritable. These conditions destroy Right Effort and gumption.

Impatience and Progress

One version of the impatience trap occurs when you constantly worry about how long it is taking you to complete a task. For instance, you have three chapters to study for an exam, and while you are reading the first chapter, you're watching the clock wondering if you will have time to finish all three before the test. You feel rushed and wish you were further along. After each page of chapter one, you turn to the end to see how many more pages you have to go.

You try to whiz through chapter one by consuming words but not digesting them. You finally finish. And ... horrors! It's chapter two. How much more can you take? If chapter one was the introductory chapter, the one that always takes it easy on you, and it took you an hour to read it, chapter two will surely take you the rest of the night to read. It's hopeless. You might as well give up. Why put yourself through this?

The cause of this impatience is twofold: (1) you did not allocate enough time for studying, and (2) you're thinking about results. Your focus is on finishing all the chapters, instead of on the process or on understanding what you are reading while you're reading it.

A good general rule is to estimate realistically the amount of time it will take you to finish an assignment and then double it. This gives you enough time to deal with the unanticipated problems and delays that always arise. In other words, you anticipate unanticipated setbacks and make time for them in planning your work sessions.

Everyone knows the importance of allocating enough time for a task. Everyone is aware of the consequences of having insufficient time to do something. The problem is that despite grasping the significance of having adequate time to do a job right many of us don't give ourselves enough time because we simply don't plan our work carefully.

Planning and Time Management

Setting aside enough time so thinking about time does not interfere with your performance requires planning and self-discipline. Obviously, it's a good idea to have a monthly calendar on which you can record significant dates, such as due dates for exams and presentations. Then, you can plan your daily activities around these dates. If your plan is realistic and you stick to it, it can go a long way in reducing impatience and anxiety. You are less likely to become worried and agitated about finishing on time, and you are more likely to become focused on what you are supposed to be doing.

In addition to planning for the month, a daily schedule is also important in managing impatience and anxiety. If you follow one, you don't have to make a decision about what to do next each time you complete a task. There will be no question about what you are going to do next, you just look at your schedule. But in order to benefit from a schedule, you have to follow it pretty strictly. Don't fall for the argument that it's probably more important for you to go for a tension reducing swim or relax by playing your favorite video game.

Schedule Slavery

You should build into your schedule ample time for meditation, breaks, leisure, and exercise. And you should be aware of falling into the trap of worrying all the time about being on schedule. In this trap, your whole day is a hectic race to get everything on your list done. As you're doing one thing, for example, a reading assignment, you're wondering if you will finish in time for your scheduled workout. While you're working out, you're constantly concerned that you won't get to your next project or class.

How do you avoid becoming a slave of your own making by shackling yourself to a schedule that destroys your gumption and keeps you in a constant state of time place dissonance? First, of course, be realistic. Don't try to do too many things in one day, and make sure to give yourself enough time to complete each activity on your schedule.

Second, each day when you write your schedule, reaffirm your commitment to do each task with Right Effort. Get yourself in the right frame of mind before you start each task. A simple way is to tell yourself before each task, "For the next X amount of time, I am going to do Y with full attention."

There will be days when you have to alter your schedule. Don't worry about it. But, make sure that you have a good reason for doing it. Never postpone a task you don't feel like doing because you think you'll feel more like doing it some other time. Let those feelings dissipate into the spaciousness of mind that you've developed through your meditation practice.

Chapter 18

Gumption Trap 7: Procrastination

We've already discussed procrastination to some extent in relation to the impatience and energy traps. However, we have not presented it in the depth it deserves. Procrastination, broadly defined, is putting off a task to the extent that it has obvious negative consequences for you.

Although the problem of procrastination is endemic in professionals and college students, there is considerable variation in the severity or intensity of the problem. Procrastinators can be divided into two categories: (1) simple-motive procrastinators who account for a substantial majority (75 percent), and (2) complex, chronic, or dysfunctional procrastinators (25 percent).[51] Each kind of procrastination

---

51   University at Buffalo, 2005

can be further subdivided. In the next sections, some of the various types of procrastination are presented. See if you are represented in any of the descriptions.

Simple Motive Procrastination: Skills and Knowledge Deficits

One of the most straightforward reasons for procrastinating is disinterest in the material. Often students find studying, writing papers, and doing academic projects distasteful.[52] In many cases, student motivation is deficient and academic performance is limited by inadequate academic skills.

Students are most likely to delay or fail to complete academic tasks that are difficult for them, consume a lot of their time, and/or require skills, talents, and knowledge they have not developed.[53] Students in these circumstances are not likely to derive any intrinsic satisfaction from working on an academic task, and because they delay doing their school work to the point where they don't have time to do a quality job, they are unlikely to learn much. These students are in a dangerous situation. If they don't learn much from one assignment, they will not develop the knowledge base and talents to do the next one.

If you fit this category, one solution is to get remedial help and/or tutorial help. This way you can get up to speed so you can face challenging academic work. If you find you are judging yourself for needing assistance, don't get engaged in a tortuous episode of self-criticism. Let negative opinions of yourself pass.

---

52   University at Buffalo, 2005

53   University at Buffalo, 2005

You know from your meditation practice that letting go of criticism sounds simple. However, when you try to put it into operation, it requires a commitment to moment-by-moment awareness to a wide range of situations. There's nothing easy about it.

Cool Procrastinator

The second kind of simple motive procrastinator is the cool procrastinator. The main characteristic of this student is a disproportionate focus on social activities.

The social scene for the cool procrastinator represents a diversion from the reality of more pressing tasks, which he may find tedious and frustrating. The cool procrastinator takes advantage of all social opportunities to create excitement and reduce tedium. This strategy actually increases procrastination. As everyone knows, too much time on the party-entertainment-social events circuit leaves little time for schoolwork.

The cool procrastinator should review his goals and reorient himself. The social scene will still call to him. But when there is work to be done, he must simply observe cravings for the social scene and get to work. Without doubt, it is a challenging solution.

Procrastination and Perceived Relevance to Career

A specific example of deficiency procrastination is perceived pertinence of college and courses to a specific career. Some college students see much of what they are asked to do in college as irrelevant to their future careers. After all, how will exposure to the plays of Shakespeare, the poetry of Keats, or Tibetan Buddhist tangka painting help them to be a better business manager or nurse? If they don't see a course as applicable to their future employment, they may come to loathe course assignments and put them off to the last minute.

If your procrastination is grounded in a lack of perceived relevance of your academic work to a certain career or job, keep three points in mind. First, the purpose of higher education is broader than training you for a specific job. Second, your career is likely to change several times during your working life so developing broad abilities with wide relevance is obviously to your benefit. Third, some research on employers indicates that they are looking to hire graduates who have general abilities (e.g., writing, analyzing, synthesizing, collaborating, and lifelong learning) rather than specific job-related skills.

Complex Motives for Procrastination

The examples of procrastination discussed so far are relatively uncomplicated. There are also complex reasons, which are more serious, long-lasting, and difficult to redress than simple procrastination. The category of complex, trait, dysfunctional, or chronic procrastinators includes: the perfectionist procrastinator and the cavalier or dismissive procrastinator.

Perfectionist Procrastinator

A study of procrastination among college students found that the factor having the strongest association with the frequency of procrastination was perfectionism.[54]

---

54   Reasinger and Brownlow, 1996

The perfectionist, let's call her Ms. Pricilla P. Perfecto, suffers from high levels of anxiety and other symptoms of discomfort. Pricilla procrastinates because she feels that she can never get things right. When she does start on a project, she delays completion because Pricilla feels everything has to be perfect before she submits it. Perfection, of course, is an unattainable goal. The perfectionist can never get everything right. Nonetheless, Ms. Pricilla P. Perfecto either tries to reach perfection and/or obsesses about attaining it. Both hinder her in finishing academic tasks. It takes Pricilla an inordinate amount of time to accomplish any major project. Even when she does complete a project, Pricilla is convinced that it is not good enough.

Cavalier Procrastinator

The cavalier procrastinator takes a flippant or sometimes even a derisive view of academic projects. On the surface he looks much like the cool procrastinator, but his problem runs deeper and it is more difficult to resolve.

Let's take a look at a cavalier procrastinator. Carlton Carefree seems to be unperturbed by assignments and exams. Academic tasks apparently don't interfere with other aspects of his life, like his numerous social activities.

He doesn't even seem to mind when he gets a bad grade. He appears to possess an astonishing level of self-confidence. He doesn't have to rely on some professor's judgment of his intelligence. He knows he's smart, especially on the street smart dimension of intelligence. If there were a valid measure of street smarts, Carlton Carefree has no doubt he would score in the 99.9th percentile. When it comes to schoolwork, he's just not willing to put in a lot of effort. There are so many other activities that are more interesting than classes and homework.

Carlton has a condescending view of many professors. They just aren't street smart, and they are the antithesis of cool. Indeed, many are utter dweebs. Some are obviously incompetent. In Carlton's view, most professors don't know their field, teach material that is irrelevant and boring, give unclear instructions and lectures, and do not grade fairly. Most have no sense of style, and some are so old they are revolting to look at. They really shouldn't be seen in public.

Commonality Between Priscilla and Carlton

At first glance, the perfectionist procrastinator and the cavalier procrastinator appear to be very different people, and in many ways they are. However, their procrastination has the same roots. They both lack self-confidence and suffer from fear of failure.

Pricilla P. Perfecto procrastinates because she thinks she is expected to do perfect work and she can't measure up. This lack of confidence and fear of failure contributes to her procrastinating, and in some situations, she becomes immobilized.

Carlton Carefree's procrastination is also grounded in low self-confidence. He doesn't feel that he can measure up, but instead of putting in extraordinary effort like Pricilla, he takes himself out of the game. If you are not in the game, you can't lose. He's in school, but he's not an academic player. He's a player in other arenas. This gambit saves face for Carlton. To fail to try and to appear not to care is better in his eyes than to try and fail.

To some extent, both Pricilla Perfecto and Carlton Carefree are caught in the ego trap. They are a variation on our old friend Student E. Monster. Their focus is on themselves and how they will look to others impedes learning and performance. Carlton Carefree does little and learns nothing because he fears the embarrassment of failure. He needs to save face. Pricilla Perfecto is so concerned about meeting high expectations that she becomes hyper-focused on the academic task to the extent that she is incapacitated by the anxiety it generates.

In both cases, self-focus takes such prominence that there is little attention and energy to apply to the academic task when they do get to it. The best solution is to increase awareness or mindfulness while gradually and gently diminishing self-focus and increasing attention to the task.

Procrastination as a Clinical Symptom

There are cases of severe procrastination that can be a symptom of a serious psychological problem. This happens most often to the perfectionist procrastinator.

If you find your procrastination immobilizing and debilitating, get to your school counseling center or a local counselor for testing and diagnosis. You shouldn't judge yourself. Getting help is not something to avoid. In some cases, mindfulness-based cognitive behavior therapy (MBCBT) can help.

19

Gumption Trap 8:
Story Land or Story Mind

We all like a good story, and we are all experts at generating them. We especially like the ones in which we are the central character. These are the ones where we are victorious, superior, or deeply loved. Sometimes we even like the ones where bad things happen as long as we have the leading role.

Stories can take a number of forms. There's pure fantasy, e.g., we are film stars, professional athletes, and Nobel Laureates in both literature and theoretical physics.

They can also take the form of past or future events. But no matter if your story is in the future or past, there is one very important thing to remember about any story. It is just a story.

Melvin M. Milquetoast Redux

Let's take a look at the contours of a story by looking at the case of Melvin M. Milquetoast. Do you remember Melvin, the beleaguered Little Leaguer? He's in his early twenties now, and with age, the situations that cause him suffering and humiliation have changed.

Three and a half weeks ago, Melvin met Helen Aphrodite, a gorgeous and talented young woman who was three-time winner of the Troy, NY Greco-Roman Filo Dough Tournament. For Melvin, Helen was "the one" or "the real thing." As natives of the West of Ireland put it, he was "arse over tea kettle" in love with her. His love for her was so strong that it clouded his otherwise impeccably rational judgment.

Melvin's Parisian cousin, Juliette Brie nee Fefe, a bona fide consultant on all things romantic, convinced him that a surprise marriage proposal party was the dream of every young woman. Everyone would simply love it.

Juliette rented O'Leary's Petite Paris Tearoom and Celtic Pub for the event. Helen was brought to O'Leary's under the pretext of an Irish wake for Melvin's best friend from childhood, Seamus O'Donnybrook. The plan was to have Melvin glide down from the ceiling in a white dove costume. He would hold a ten karat diamond ring in his beak and ask Helen if she would take his wing in marriage. He had practiced talking with a ring in his beak for weeks to make his delivery audible.

On cue, Melvin came diving not gliding from the center beam of the ceiling. Neither Melvin nor his cousin Juliette was aware that costume dove wings didn't allow you to glide or fly. Melvin crashed into the table of honor; the force made him swallow the ring; his dove head detached bouncing over to the closed casket; it hit a lever opening the casket releasing hundreds of Mister Happy Face balloons along with a dozen or so live white doves, actually they were pigeons covered in white theatrical paint. Half of the balloons burst, and several doves/pigeons died of helium gas poisoning. Melvin sat on the floor sobbing and flapping his useless dove wings.

It was pandemonium. Someone called the fire department. Many guests were plastered against the wall by the force of the water from the fire hoses. Others crawled out doors and windows. A beefcake bartender, Dan O'Connell, carrying a bottle of Jameson Irish Whiskey was groping Helen as he escorted her out the employee's door to the safety the Kilgore Trout Hourly Hotel and Spa. Rumor has it that Helen and Dan were married that day by Reverend Kilgore Trout.

This is the kind of story that endures and evolves. It contains strong emotions such as love. It doesn't get any stronger than that. There's also humiliation, betrayal, and second guesses about many decisions. There are numerous junctures at which hypothetical alternatives can be explored. How would it have changed things if Melvin's dove wings had worked? What if the bartender had been a hideously ugly, odious, foul-smelling carny? Would it have worked better if Melvin wore a crow costume?

Melvin could spend considerable time and mental energy examining these questions and others. He'd find that investigating one question leads to considering variants on it and prompts others. Melvin's inquiry about the incident could last the rest of his life. He could find himself living most of his life in the past. Very little of his life will be spent in the present, which is the only place life can truly be lived. Even when Melvin makes a great effort to force himself to live in the reality of the present, he will find the story of his engagement irresistible.

Melvin's story of his engagement party can also affect future stories or fantasies. Stories of retaliation are especially frequent in cases in which humiliation and infidelity are factors like Melvin's.

His recurring future fantasies reflect the theme of random encounters in New York City with Helen and Dan. In one story, Melvin runs into Helen and Dan on East 84th St. in Manhattan. While greeting the couple, Melvin notices that they both look just a bit down at the heel. They are still an attractive couple despite wearing hardly noticeable shabby clothes. Melvin is wearing a handmade, dapper suit with monogramed sharkskin boots.

Melvin greets Helen and Dan, and they make small talk. They ask if Melvin is married. They assume Melvin is lonely as a lifelong bachelor. No one could take Helen's place after she left him a broken man in a dove costume. Just then a sizzling hot, strawberry blonde driving a Lamborghini pulls to the curb and signals to Melvin to hop in. Melvin quickly introduces her as his wife, Roxanne, to Helen and Dan. Melvin jumps into the car and they go cruising past the Met down Fifth Ave.

Another story reflecting the common theme is Roxanne and Melvin volunteer in a soup kitchen on Thanksgiving and serve Helen and Dan. Still another is Melvin and Roxanne rescue Helen and Dan on the West Side from a group of Irish hooligans affiliated with the notorious Irish gang the Westies. When asked what they were doing in the Hell's Kitchen area of New York, the turf of the Westies, Dan admits that they were trying to score drugs.

By now you get the picture. There are plenty of compelling stories to engage Melvin. By the way, Melvin was a lonely bachelor who pined for Helen. He worked as a bike courier in Manhattan and died on the job when he rode into a utility pole. He was involved in a Helen story at the time and not paying attention to where he was going. Melvin's last words were "I hope that was Dan O'Connell I hit." His wake was held at O'Leary's Petite Paris Tearoom and Celtic Pub. Reverend Kilgore Trout officiated.

The way to deal with stories is the same as you deal with everything else that draws you away from the present. As soon as you realize you are involved in a story, label it story or the particular theme or topic of the story, let it be, and get back into the present.

Stories are complex and persistent. Many are recurring and it brings temporary comfort to play the story lines or run head-movies. You have to remind yourself that they are not real; they are not in the present. The more you practice staying in the moment, the better you'll get at recognizing stories as they arise, noting they are not real, and getting back to the present.

There's no question that stories are captivating and a major distraction when you meditate or practice mindfulness in any way. For some of us, a first step in dealing with them is to reframe our stories. You can see stories as an invitation or opportunity to practice mindfulness. The obstacles to awareness of the moment are transformed into a way to develop your mindfulness.

If Melvin had followed the prescription for handling stories perhaps he would be with us today.

Chapter 20

Gumption Trap 9:
The Big Wombassa

We've saved the Big Wombassa for last because it's so pervasive and recurrent in most of our lives. The term was first introduced by John Brockman[55], editor of *Edge: The Third Culture*. You should stay on high alert for this gumption draining fiend, and be ready to deal with it again and again.

The Big Wombassa emerges when we cling to the notion that there is some future point in our lives where everything will be ok and all will fall into place. This is an imagined place in life where we will finally get all that we want and need to be happy for the rest of our lives. It's typically linked to an event or development in life that we see as defining the beginning of our idea of living life as it really should be lived. We consider it the start of our "real life."

55   Brockman, 2004

The problem is that it's an illusion. There is no event, development, or point in time that ushers in our personal era of complete and permanent contentment. Thinking that there is such a time or situation sets us up for disappointment, frustration, and resentment.

Most of us have experienced the anticipation-disappointment cycle or the Big Wombassa many times. We can recall dozens of times when we have gotten what we want or think we need for total satisfaction in life only to find that it's not as we thought it would be. Yet, we remain firm believers that our day of complete fulfillment will come.

Many of us spend our entire lives waiting for our "real life" to begin. It's always about to happen when we reach the next milestone. For instance, our "real life" will begin when we go to college... graduate from college... start a promising career... get married...buy a house... have children... send the children to college... retire...Inevitably, we die, and our "real life" on earth for this round never occurs. Our real life, which is our only life in this body or form, is the life we have this very moment. When we're in college, our real life is going to school. When we retire, our real life is being retired. It's more than recognition of our identity with a stage, state, or event in life. It's immersion in the life we are living right now.

The bulk of the research evidence indicates that most of us don't do a very good job of "affective forecasting" or predicting how good we'll feel for how long when we get what we want or a desirable event occurs. We suffer from "impact bias" or the tendency to overestimate our emotional response to future events.[56] We anticipate that if certain things happen in our lives, e.g., a new job, a new love, winning the big game, or hitting the lottery, we will

---

56   Wilson and Gilbert, 2005

be happier for a longer period of time than we actually are when those things do occur. The difference between the level and duration of our anticipated happiness and actual or experienced happiness indicates the magnitude of our disappointment or disenchantment. The bigger the gap the more we've been crushed by the Big Wombassa.

The good news is that you have a substantial amount of control over the shape your real life takes. You set the goals that largely determine your day-to-day activities, and you can learn how to pay attention and put mindfulness into operation in all that you do to attain your goals. Through present awareness of what you are doing, you experience the intrinsic satisfaction of each moment. The satisfaction that comes from your life right now is more likely to result in a permanent increase in happiness than waiting for your life circumstances to change. You experience this satisfaction repeatedly as long as you pay attention. It's the only way to escape the clutches of the Big Wombassa.

One way to hold onto your dreams but deal effectively with the Big Wombassa is to face it. While following the path to your goals, keep in mind that when you get to your destination, it may not be what you envisioned. Ants will still join you on the perfect picnics you planned. Petals will fall from even the most pampered roses. Nevertheless, your dreams will be recognizable in the context of the reality. Besides, if you stay open to your circumstances, you may find harmony and inspiration in industrious ants and melancholy beauty in dead rose petals.

Chapter 21

General Gumption Conservation and Restoration Methods

Techniques for restoring gumption and avoiding the depletion of gumption were presented in relation to some of the specific gumption traps covered so far. The general method for handling most of these traps is some variation on foundations of meditation and mindfulness: (1) monitoring, staying alert, or paying attention; (2) recognizing when your mind wanders; (3) observing and letting be or witnessing and letting go of thoughts, feelings, and sensations that take you out of the moment; and (4) gently returning to the present moment.

The general techniques described in this section can be used in response to a variety of the gumption traps we've covered. They may also be applicable to areas that we have not explicitly addressed.

Technique 1: Bagging

People who suffer from excessive worry (and other recurring emotions and thoughts) have found the bagging technique helpful. Worriers are instructed to designate one period of their day, from a few minutes to a half-hour, to worry. During the designated time, they can worry as much as they want. At other times of the day, however, they are instructed to put worries aside. They must postpone worrying or "bag it" until the designated time. Some people have found that it is helpful to visualize putting their worries into a bag; tying it; and opening it at the appropriate time.

If you use the bagging technique, you will often find when you open your bag at the designated time that your previous feelings and thoughts have lost much of their force. Indeed, some may seem silly when they are no longer closely tied to their original context. If, however, they were allowed to attach to the original event rather than being put aside, they would have interfered with your task performance.

Bagging should not be confused with suppression of emotions. You are not bottling up your feelings. You are recognizing your feelings, and placing them in the bag where they are retrievable. You are setting aside your feelings. You recognize that a particular feeling has arrived, but you postpone engagement so you don't interfere with focusing on your present activity.

When you open the bag at the designated time, invite the contents to reenter your inner world. Welcome whatever is in the bag. Be open to thoughts and emotions. Feel them; and experience them as fully as possible. Make inquiries. Where do you feel anxiety? Is it in your stomach? Is it in your neck and shoulders? Do you feel anxiety in your chest? Where in your body is dread expressed? How about frustration? Such inquiry can lessen the impact of such emotions; they often lose their force when they are broken down further.

After you have taken the feelings and thoughts out of the bag where you have temporarily put them, just be with them. Observe them. Listen to them. Bear witness to them. But don't evaluate them or try to figure them out. Most of all, don't judge yourself for having them.

Technique 2: Relaxation

The best body-mind state for effective performance of just about anything is alert relaxation. In this state, you are aware of what you are doing and you have the mental flexibility necessary to respond to changes.

Anxiety, boredom, and other emotions produce tension. It results in a loss of the openness and flexibility necessary to recognize changes and to respond to them. As tension increases, your awareness narrows. Your attention becomes centered on the strain you feel instead of on what you are supposed to be doing. You lose touch with the present moment. You've lost track of quality. There is no rightness in your effort. You become impatient. The tension amplifies. You stop working or quit the game. You give up. But the tension remains. And now, it's tinged with guilt. Your neck is tied in knots. You feel the tension in your shoulders and back. There is pressure in your head. Your body cries out for relief.

You're in luck. Hundreds of techniques have been practiced for centuries as methods for reducing tension and producing relaxation. They help you dissolve the barriers created by tension that form between you and your work.

Relaxation techniques can go a long way in getting you back into the flow of the task or activity of the moment.

Many authors have suggested variations on a simple form of relaxation, i.e., single breath meditation. You can do it inconspicuously anywhere and at any time. One way to do it is to inhale deeply through your nose while visualizing soothing air entering your body and mind. Feel it flow through your entire body. As you exhale through your nose, feel the tension released and replaced by a state of relaxation. As with any of the relaxation practices, the keys are awareness, spaciousness, and letting go. This technique is particularly well suited for situations where it would be unreasonable to take a longer break from the task (e.g., exams or meetings). When you can afford more time, there are others.

Technique 3: Exercise

Most of us are familiar with the positive benefits of exercise on physical health, but it is also a technique for reducing psychological stress. It is especially effective in addressing some problems like anxiety and depression.[57] Frank Hu, an epidemiologist at the Harvard School of Public Health, observes, "The single thing that comes close to a magic bullet in terms of its strong and universal benefits is exercise."[58]

Despite the benefits of exercise, many of us find it difficult to establish an exercise program. The problem most of us face is finding time to make exercise a routine practice. One solution is to just fit it in whenever possible. It's well worth the effort.

---

57   See Begley, 2007
58   Hu quoted in Brody, April 29, 2008

Working out is a major commitment. Various forms of group exercise, e.g., aerobics class or a team sport may make it easier to maintain an exercise program. Finding several activities you enjoy will help to sustain motivation and interest. You don't have to be slave to a treadmill or pumping iron. You can hike, do yoga, or dance with someone other than your books.

Frank Zane, three time Mr. Olympia and longtime meditation advocate, stresses the most important aspect of exercise is to do it mindfully. If your exercise is walking your dog every day, and it's all that you can do, do it with all the attention or awareness you can bring to it. The way to approach your exercise program is the way we suggest for approaching all worthwhile activities. Make the commitment and do it with Right Effort. Focus on process not goals. When you exercise, just exercise.

Technique 4: The Study Group or Book Dance

Group support has long been recognized as an effective way to promote and maintain changes in values, attitudes, and behaviors. Many structured, repetitive activities that require considerable discipline are performed in groups. Not only are many forms of meditation done in groups, but also some kinds of dance, yoga, and martial arts.

The study group is hardly a novel idea. It is a form of cooperative learning that has a powerful positive influence. Traditional study groups are generally focused on a specific subject or course. The study group envisioned here will focus not only on content or the subject matter of a course, but also on the method or process of studying. You can even have a study group where individual group members study for different courses for a specific period of time and then discuss the process of studying. The kind of study group we are suggesting is a collective book dance, which, of course, promotes Dancing With Your Books.

The study group presented below is a group with a specific structure and procedures. It's not the same as simple group study where students get together to study without any formal organization or direction. This kind of collective study has been found to have no influence on the development of important academic abilities such as critical thinking skills. Indeed, individual study contributes more than unstructured group study.[59]

The exact practices followed by a group will depend on its composition. But all groups should consider including short periods of sitting and/or walking meditation. Members should agree to meet at the same time several days a week. Ideally, meetings should last at least two hours. The group should maintain silence during study and meditation. Discussions about the process of study should be held at the end of study session.

It's important to establish most of the group policies and rules at the first meeting. Group conventions should be developed concerning (1) the use of cell phones (e.g., they should be turned off during meeting times or only used during specified periods), (2) attendance (e.g., members will be dropped from the group if they miss a specified number of meetings unless for extraordinary reasons), (3) punctuality, (4) staying on task during meetings, and (5) any other issues group members see as important.

Attendance at study sessions and participation in the book dance are serious matters. The absence of any group member can undermine the commitment of fellow members and drain gumption. Each member should consider

---

59   Arum and Roksa, 2010

participation an important obligation. It is a demonstration of dedication and caring.

A group facilitator or discussion leader should be assigned on a rotating basis for each week. The purpose of the facilitator is to keep the group on task. Without a facilitator's guidance, discussions can become merely a time for socializing or worse, a gripe session.

In addition to tactfully keeping the group on the subject during the discussions, the facilitator should remind group members of the time and place of meetings via email, call, text, tweet, group website, or other methods. The facilitator is also responsible for selecting and presenting a discussion of a study/learning topic for the week.

When it is their turn to be group facilitator, each member will have the chance to practice their presentation skills in what should be a comfortable and supportive environment. This is an important benefit of being in a group and a reason that no one should be allowed to skip being facilitator.

The group facilitator can choose from a broad range of topics for discussion of the process and method of study. These may include suggestions or techniques presented in this book or those garnered from other books, lectures, or classes. Some examples of discussion topics are (1) dealing with boredom, (2) getting out of your own way, (3) preparing for a test, (4) time management, and (5) the cost and benefits of studying while driving.

The weekly facilitator should become the group's expert on a particular topic or set of topics. At least once during any week, the facilitator should do a formal presentation on the topic. For the remainder of the week, the group can discuss the topic, problem, or issue selected by the facilitator. The central purpose of the discussion is so members of the group can share insights, problems, and discoveries related to putting suggestions or techniques related to the topic into practice. The discussion of the particular topic should continue from meeting to meeting until the end of the week or until most members feel that they have exhausted the topic. If the discussion stops before the end of the week, open discussions on other relevant subjects can be held at the conclusion of each study session.

The size of the group is an important issue. The study group is not a club that tries to attract as many members as possible. The study group should not be more than six members. In larger groups, some people get lost, and not everyone gets the chance to participate.

One way to promote commitment to the group and its objectives is to establish a group identity by giving your study group a name, for example, the Douglass College Book Ballet Company. You might also consider performing group rituals at each meeting as a method of reaffirming your commitment and to help members loosen up and relax. Here we're not suggesting that you eat peyote buttons and sacrifice a professor or two to the study gods before each study session. Bowing to each other and/or reciting a set of affirmations is ritualistic enough for some groups. If your group is more adventuresome, you might choreograph and perform a short group dance.

Transformation of a Wallflower: A Digression

Allow us to digress for a moment to explain the last recommendation, i.e., group dance. We know it may sound a little bizarre to some of you.

This idea is based on an experience the elder author, Jake, had many years ago so it will be presented in the first person.

I was attending a weekend introductory session at Kripalu Center for Yoga & Health in Lenox, MA (www.kripalu.org) with my wife, Kate, her older sister, Mary Ellen, to whom we dedicated the book, and Marty, the guy mentioned earlier who introduced me to the idea of staying in the moment, and then didn't remember it.

Kate, Mary Ellen, and Marty considered the weekend an opportunity to catch up on their sleep and get a few different kinds of massages. My insomnia precluded the "sleep through the weekend" option, so I went to a variety of sessions that were introductions to yoga, bodywork, relaxation techniques, and so on.

I went to one memorable activity in a room about the size of a junior high school gym. There was a guy in the front beating a drum, and the attendees were instructed to dance. That was it. No one showed us how to dance. We were just supposed to start dancing. So, we did.

We started to dance in all different kinds of ways. Soon after we started, just about all of us were dancing in groups. The groups would form; people would dance together for a few minutes; and participants would dance around to form new groups.

At first, I felt really silly. I could feel myself blushing. I think if I had been near the door, I would have danced on out. But I gave it a short try, and it wasn't long before I felt a sense of joyous relaxation and liberation. Surprisingly, I found that I was not a bit self-conscious. I don't think this had ever happened to me before in my life while dancing. I was actually having fun. It looked like everyone else was, too. I experienced a sense of calm and light heartedness for hours after the dance session. It would be a great state to be in when approaching any task, including studying.

Technique 5: Bowing and Bells

The practice of bowing, which is uncommon in contemporary Western culture, also helps you to pay full attention to the task or activity of the moment. A bow before beginning a task symbolizes that you have deep respect for it and you intend to devote your full attention to it. When you bow, it means that you are putting all else behind you, and you are clearing your mind for the activity of the moment. You are surrendering to what needs to be done. When you bow into an activity, you are honoring it. You are showing reverence for your life in the present moment.

A bow at the end of a task is a way of clearing the mind and completely leaving the task in preparation for full absorption in the next task. It helps you develop the ability to move entirely from task to task.

You will find that if you approach each task with Right Effort, your bow will feel very natural. It will never feel forced or strained. If you are in a public place, just a subtle nod of your head will serve as your bow.

Ringing a bell serves a purpose similar to the bow. Meditation periods are started and ended with the ringing of a bell at many meditation retreats. The ringing at the beginning of a task is a call to the present moment and the task to be done. The ringing at the end signifies the task has ended, and it is time to relax into the present moment before starting on your next task. Take a few breaths to relax and refresh your mind before you move onto the next activity on your schedule.

Your bowing or ringing is emblematic of your commitment to the practice of Right Effort. They are ways to remind yourself that each task is an end in itself and not just a means to an end.

Technique 6: The Half Smile

Smiling is another simple technique that has restorative power.[60] You don't need the kind of full smile you exhibit when you're just thrilled to meet somebody or good fortune has smiled upon you and you're smiling back. A subtle half smile can restore your gumption when you are frustrated, down, or you have lost your mindfulness.

Research supports the idea that smiling has invigorating qualities. It relaxes facial muscles and has a positive effect on the nervous system. Try a half smile for a few minutes and see what happens.

Remember, this isn't an ear-to-ear smile where you go about your business with what will appear to others to be an insane grin on your face. It also isn't the kind of cynical smile we've all encountered when someone questions the credibility of what we are telling them. It's just a faint smile that acts to reinitiate mindfulness in what we are doing.

Technique 7: Creating A Bigger Container/Spaciousness

One way to look at expanding awareness is creating more spaciousness[61] or a bigger container.[62] Intrusive thoughts

---

60   Bodian, 2006

61   Packer, 1990

62   Beck, 1989

and other obstacles may still enter your mind at a rapid-fire pace, but with increased spaciousness or mind-space, you provide more room for them. This results in reducing their power to drag you around.

In a smaller container or internal space, one thought coming to mind can change everything. Take the case of Vito "Tiny" Bertillino. Tiny is a 6'6", 250 lb. defensive lineman of the Whatsamatta U. football team in Frostbite Falls, MI. Tiny is a large man with a small container.[63]

We find Tiny before practice cooking along on an assigned chemistry project when the thought that his dog, Venus, doesn't love him as much as he loves her appears in his mind. In a small container, a thought as powerful as questioning his dog's love overwhelms everything else in his mind-space and forces him to stop working on the chemistry project.

As soon as Tiny questions his dog's love, a series of related questions try to push their way into his mind-space. Does Venus really love him, or is she just in it for those cute, little drumstick treats from genetically engineered tiny chickens? How does he measure the depth of his dog's love? Is it in her eyes? Is it in her kiss? Is it in her tail? Is Venus letting someone else scratch her belly?

In a larger space, a thought even as powerful as the question of his dog's love would not have the ability to take over the entire space of Tiny's mind. It would not push everything else aside. There would be room to accommodate his thoughts and resulting feelings about his dog along with other thoughts. If Tiny were working with a bigger container, he would have room for a relatively large number

---

63   Whatsamatter U. in Frostbite Falls, MI is where Bullwinkle Moose went to school and played football on the Rocky and His Friends cartoon.

and variety of thoughts, feelings, and sensations.

How does Tiny get a bigger container or a more spacious mind? There are two ways. The first is conceptual and temporary. Tiny can imagine his mind-space expanding to a size large enough to contain questions about his dog's affection and his chemistry project. This way his container will not be filled by thoughts of Venus. He can accommodate them in his bigger container and get back to his school work.

If Tiny has a meditation practice, it will also create a bigger container. This second way creates a more permanent expansion. With a mediation practice, Tiny may eventually have enough space to handle potent thoughts and feelings and stay on the task at hand.

Spaciousness or a bigger container gives Tiny a different perspective on life events. More space gives him a broader view, a bigger picture. It makes it less likely that he will *react*, or overreact, to events of the moment, and more likely that he will *respond* appropriately. Destructive thoughts and negative emotions that arise from a variety of sources are more likely to be "kept in perspective" when they are given more room. Tiny can simply note them, and give them some space. He can afford it when he has plenty of space available.

A bigger container will help Tiny learn that thoughts are just thoughts. Some are constructive and true, others are erroneous and unlikely. Whatever the thoughts may be, with a spacious enough container, Tiny will have room for all of them, and bring his attention back to the task he should be focusing on.

Increased Response Time

As we've already seen, a bigger container or more spaciousness is one aspect of awareness that develops through meditation. Another aspect of mindfulness that is important for staying on task, or staying in the moment, is getting better at recognizing obstacles to settling into the present moment as they arise.

As we all know, irrelevant thoughts often arise while we are doing schoolwork, and they take us light years away from what we should be doing. Our minds drift to other times and places when we are supposed to be paying attention to what we are doing. We get engaged in a thought-feeling-sensation episode or a story. Before we know it, we are deeply involved in something that has little or nothing to do with the task at hand. We've been derailed by our own mind.

As our awareness develops, we are able to recognize intrusive thoughts and feelings for what they are shortly after they arise. We simply observe them and release them into the spaciousness of our bigger container. It's the mindful version of "catch and release." We become more skilled at catching disruptive thoughts, emotions, and sensations before they get rolling or roiling.

Technique 8: The Snow Globe

The snow globe is a visualization technique that can be used to promote clarity. Start by imagining whatever is limiting your gumption as whirling snowflakes in a snow globe that has been shaken. Watch the flakes that represent your gumption-draining emotions and thoughts settle to the bottom of the globe. Your vision is now crystal clear to see where you are and what you should be doing.[64]

---

64   Das, 2011

Technique 9: Daily Affirmations

One way to start your day with gumption is to recite a list of affirmations that reflect the behaviors and attitudes required to carry out your day with Right Effort. Recitation of the basic tenets of a philosophy or approach to life is commonly heard in groups, programs, and organizations that are devoted to personal growth. For example, in some traditional karate dojos, training sessions begin and/or end with a spirited group recitation of principles by which one should train and live— for instance, train earnestly with creativity; be humble and polite; do not be too proud or modest; be calm and swift; live a plain life.

An affirmation used in the sense described here is not wishful, unrealistic, or magical thinking. Affirmations are not rules that you must follow or face self-reproach. Affirmations are simply a method for establishing intention and commitment.

You can develop your own set of statements to reflect the principles by which you want to conduct your life. By reciting them each morning, you reaffirm your commitment to live by your principles. Here is one short set of reminders:

- Be kind to yourself, no matter what.
- Accept events and circumstances.
- Live in the present.
- Don't take things personally.
- Accept the past.
- Don't dwell on yourself.
- Let go.
- Don't worry about personal gain.
- Do not speak out of anger.
- Do not criticize others.
- Do everything with Right Effort.

Lists of affirmations are not only useful at the beginning of your day but can also be used throughout the day when you notice that your gumption supply is getting low. Whenever you feel your enthusiasm fade or your involvement in the moment diminish, take a break and review your list.

Short inspirational quotations from your favorite authors can also be used to help restore gumption. Keep a small notebook in which some of your favorite passages are copied, and refer to them when you feel the need.

Technique 10: The 95MPH Cornball Pitch

No matter how we try to say it, the message we will struggle to convey in this section sounds corny and mushy. It could strike you as the quintessential statement of simple sentimentality concerning the self. Yet, it is a powerful message that is consistently found in various forms in wisdom and inspirational literature. The message is: "Love yourself."

Loving yourself is not the self-aggrandizement of the dysfunction ego of Professor Monster Ego. It does not mean you should become vain and self-centered.

Loving yourself means self-acceptance. Here the word love means "...nonjudgmental caring. That kind of love grows only through developing the ability to listen and to understand deeply."[65] To love yourself, you listen carefully to your authentic voice and see clearly who you are with all your faults and failings.

Loving yourself requires that you accept whatever has happened in your past and what you think and feel in the present. If you are anxious, love, accept, or surrender to

65   Alexander, 1997, p. 8

the anxious you, and get on with the task at hand. Don't resist. Accept whatever you are in the Now.

A component of loving yourself is self-compassion. Researchers have found in studies of physicians and others that self-compassion contributes to maintaining interest in what you're doing and doing a quality job.[66]

Giving yourself a break or accepting your mistakes and shortcomings is the polar opposite of the conventional approach. Since childhood we have been taught an aggressive or Rambo strategy for dealing with our limitations. The threat of self-criticism, self-censure, or self-scorn if we do not measure up, make a mistake, or fail, is considered a powerful deterrent or disincentive to doing things wrong and a compelling motivator or incentive for doing things right.

Obviously, employing self-criticism to shape our behavior has a paradoxical effect. It's just the opposite of what we have come to expect. Instead of diminishing the chances of failure, it increases them.

An antidote to this problem is to suspend the critical function and accept who you are wherever you are doing whatever you are doing. Let yourself be you and get on with what you have to do. Adding self-criticism to what you're doing takes some of your attention away from your effort in the present and increases the chances you will fail.

Some people like Student E. Monster are in a perpetual state of self-censure and self-contempt. E. Monster and many others are terrified by the thought of just being themselves. They can't find much to like in themselves, and they are convinced that if they were just themselves, other people wouldn't like them. They often feel unwor-

---

66   Parker-Pope, 2011

thy and undeserving. Sometimes people who are quite successful by conventional standards seem to be in an unrelenting state of self-criticism, and they are convinced that they are frauds who mislead others. They feel they don't merit their success, and that they will eventually be found out.

Whenever you start to feel the "uns" (e.g., unworthy, unwholesome, unsuccessful, uninspired, and/or unloved), relax and center yourself by counting a few breaths. Reflect for a moment on the thought that you must accept whatever you were in the past and you have a duty to try to do your best in the present. Let yourself be. Accept what you see with kindness and understanding. This is the most that you or anyone else should expect of you.

Chapter 22

What's Next and What Isn't

The next part of the book is the conclusion and summary. As with most books, this part wraps things up and reviews some of the important information presented in the book.

Before we move on to the conclusion, we'd like to briefly present some areas that we didn't cover. Many of these topics are typically discussed in "how to books" that help students improve their learning ability and feature extensive treatment of academic skills, tasks, and habits. These are the nuts and bolts needed for success in getting an education. Topics include reading, writing, listening, testing, note taking, organization, planning, research, electronic literacy, critical thinking, and many more.

Authors show that academic skills not only lead to effective academic performance but also the role they play in the employment market. Skills like cogent and concise written and oral communication and creative problem solving are essential for job performance and career development. Many books contain discussions of how increasingly rapid changes in global, social, political, economic, and technological environments mean significant shifts in employment. Adapting to these changes requires unprecedented and extensive modification in the nature and delivery of education.

The major reason many of these topics are not examined in this book is that they have been presented well in a number of other books and courses. We highly recommend that you refer to books and websites on study skills and look into available courses at your school. Academic skills are essential not only for success in college, but also for lifelong learning. Knowing them will increase your effectiveness and reduce stress.

A single book can never cover all related topics. Yes, this book is about higher education, but it focuses exclusively on an effective approach to learning, i.e., the mindful approach. Topics beyond mindfulness, Right Effort, and DWB are mostly left to others. We will, however, provide additional information on the book's website, www.mindfulwaytostudy.com, where we present additional educational skills and techniques that we think are most important. We will also discuss additional topics, such as philosophy of education, the cost of college, and new developments in mindfulness. Please take a look occasionally and contribute your views to the discussion.

Part III

End and Beginning

Chapter 23

Learning with Right Effort: A Review

L earning with Right Effort or gumption merely requires that you relax into the moment and focus naturally and exclusively on the task at hand. Achieving this state of quality effort or flow, however, is a major challenge that requires a lifetime of patience, practice, and persistence.

The steps, suggestions, reminders, and pointers listed in this section are intended to help you learn with Right Effort. After you have practiced Right Effort for a while, you can develop your own list that is specifically suited just to you. In the meantime, try the following list or related suggestions for starters.

1. *Clear*: Clear your mind by doing meditation or cleansing breaths for a few minutes. You are not trying to achieve a particular state of mind. You are not trying to push anything out of mind. You are just letting things settle.

2. *Relax*: Feel your mind relax. Feel your mind open. Prepare your mind to accept whatever you are about to learn or whatever you are about to do.

3. *"Beginner's Mind"*: Find your beginner's mind. Let go of expectations. Prepare to go on a journey to a place you have never been where you will learn something new and valuable. Forget about the destination. It's the trip itself that's important. Don't worry about goals and results. Focus on process.

4. *Commitment*: Make an explicit commitment to yourself to do your work with Right Effort for a set amount of time or until you finish certain tasks. Promise yourself that you will focus exclusively on what is in front of you. Let go of other times, places, and tasks. Convince yourself that the only proper thing to do in the allotted time is what you are supposed to be doing. Don't give yourself the choice of doing anything else.

5. *Acceptance*: Accept that you have to be where you are, doing what you are doing. Right now there is no place you can be other than where you are.

6. *Absorption*: Settle into doing what you are doing. Invest yourself in each moment. Sink into it. Absorb and be absorbed by the task at hand. Surrender to the task. Embrace your books as your partner in the dance of learning.

7. *Stay in the "Now"*: Stay centered in the moment and the task at hand. When you notice that your thoughts are straying from your current task to other times and places, let go, and gently return your mind to your work.

8. *No Separation*: There is no separate self and task or person-task distinction. You and your books are inseparably melded in the task of the moment. Thoughts of a separate you working on the task only get in the way. The real you right now is the one intimately involved in whatever you are doing.

9. *Basics of Mindfulness:* Remember to follow the general process of meditation, mindfulness, or Right Effort. This includes: (1) monitoring, staying alert, or paying attention; (2) recognizing when your mind wanders; (3) observing and letting be or witnessing and letting go of thoughts, feelings, and sensations that take you out of the moment; and (4) gently returning to the present moment.

10. *Purpose*: Work as if it's the only reason you were put on this earth. Remember that right now, in this moment, is the only time there is.

After you have been trying to learn with Right Effort or gumption for a while, you should conduct a self-assessment to determine which particular impediment interferes most with your application of Right Effort. You should include as part of your daily routine the technique or techniques described in this book that address your particular set of problems.

Sticking to a daily routine is not easy. At one time or another, doubts will surface, and you will question the purpose of what you are doing. There may be some backsliding where you miss days of following your routine. You will tend to regress to your old ways, especially when you are under a lot of pressure or no pressure at all. During these times, it is particularly important to follow your program. If you get through the hard times with Right Effort, it will go a long way in strengthening your commitment to living fully with gumption.

Chapter 24

Parting Words

The late Dainin Katagiri, abbot of the Minnesota Zen Meditation Center, told his students: "If you sit zazen, zazen is your life, whether you like it or not. When you study literature, literature is life itself. When you study science, science must be burning the flame of life."[67] This simple message is the central point of this book. The only advice offered is that when you are doing something, do only that thing. Everything else written between the covers of this book is intended to help you to put this simple advice into practice, which is an immensely difficult but worthwhile challenge.

---

67   Katagiri 1988, p. 27

The Ultimate Concern

In *Buddhism Without Beliefs: A Contemporary Guide to Awakening*, Stephen Batchelor suggests the central question of our lives should be *"Since death alone is certain and the time of death uncertain, what should I do?"*[68] The obvious answer to this question is to live in the moment and do everything with Right Effort. It is the way to quality, flow, and intrinsic satisfaction in all we do.

Meditation helps to uncover what is blocking you from living in the prescribed way. Whatever else you do you should practice it every day, if possible. You may eventually experience a deep comprehension, intuition, or realization of what it means to live in the moment rather than just an intellectual understanding. A firm conceptual grasp, however, can help us along the way. We hope by now that the usefulness of a meditation practice goes without saying.

Mindfulness Beyond Education

Most of this book explored the application of mindfulness to learning. As we've noted before, mindfulness is a way of life and it's a lifelong practice. It's especially important in a world where lifelong learning is necessary to be successful. Dedication and commitment are essential to develop full awareness and they are necessary for developing a broader perspective on life and a higher level of consciousness.

Our hope is that this book has enriched your life as a student. But please, take what you have learned and extend it to all aspects of your life.

---

68   Batchelor, 1997, p. 29

May the jewel of the lotus descend into your heart.

About The Authors

Jake J. Gibbs, PhD, is an emeritus professor at Indiana University of Pennsylvania (IUP). He taught for a combined 30+ years at Rutgers University and IUP. Jake was awarded a Contemplative Practice Fellow by the Center for Contemplative Mind in Society and he is a Founding Member of the Integral Institute. His publications have appeared in the Peace Review and the AQAL: Journal of Integral Theory and Practice.

Roddy O. Gibbs is a graduate of the Psychology Honors Program at Indiana University of Pennsylvania. After graduation, Roddy took a break from higher education to pursue business ventures in San Diego, California. More importantly, Roddy developed a further interest in mindfulness and meditation while living in San Diego where he has joined a number of organizations and programs to continue the development of his practice.

Bibliography

Aitken, Robert. *Taking the Path of Zen*. San Francisco, CA: North Point, 1982.

Alexander, William. *Cool Water: Alcoholism, Mindfulness and Ordinary Recovery*. Boston, MA: Shambhala, 1997.

Amabile, Teresa. *Unleashing Creativity*. San Jose, CA: Strategies Institute Revolutionaries.

Arum, Richard, and Josipa Roksa. *Academically Adrift: Limited Learning on College Campuses*. Chicago: University of Chicago Press, 2010.

Association for Contemplative Mind in Higher Education, http://www.acmhe.org/, January, 30, 2013.

Aubrey, Allison. "Science Explores Meditation's Effect on the Brain" *Morning Edition*, National Public Radio, July 26, 2006, http://www.npr.org/templates/story/story.php?storyId=4770779.

Batchelor, Stephen. *Buddhism without Beliefs: A Contemporary Guide to Awakening*. New York: Riverhead Books, 1997.

Beck, Charlotte Joko. *Everyday Zen: Love and Work*. San Francisco, CA: Harper and Row, 1989.

Beck, Charlotte Joko with Steve Smith. *Nothing Special: Living Zen*. New York: Harper-Collins, 1993.

Begley, Sharon. *Train your Mind, Change your Brain.* New York: Ballantine, 2007.

Benoit, Hubert, *The Supreme Doctrine: Psychological Encounters in Zen Thought.* New York: Inner Traditions International, 1955.

Berger, K.T. *Zen Driving.* New York: Ballantine, 1988.

Blackburn, Dan, and Maryann Jorgenson. *Zen and The Crosscountry Skier.* Pasadena, CA: Ward Ritchie, 1976.

Bodian, Stephan. *Meditation for Dummies* (2nd ed.). Hoboken, NJ: Wiley, 2006.

Boorstein, Sylvia. *It's Easier Than You Think: The Buddhist Way to Happiness.* New York: Harper-Collins, 1995.

Brandon, David. *Zen in the Art of Helping.* New York: Dell, 1976.

Brockman, John. "Introduction to Affective Forecasting...or...the 'Big Wombassa': What You Think You're Going to Get, and What You Don't Get, When You Get What You Want: A Talk with Daniel Gilbert." *Edge: The Third Culture,* February 12, 2004, http://www.edge.org/documents/archive/edge134.html.

Brody, Jane. "You Name It and Exercise Helps It." *New York Times,* April 29, 2008.

Bush, Mirabai. "Knowing Every Breath You Take." *New York Times.* http://www.nytimes.com/2013/01/06/jobs/teaching-meditation-techniques-to-organizations.html?emc=tnt&tntemail1=y. January 5, 2013.

California Polytechnic State University, San Luis Obispo. "Procrastination." Academic Skills Center-Study Skill Library, 2006, http://www.sas.calpoly.edu/asc/ssl/procrasination/html.

Campbell, Mindy, "Living in the Here and Now: Meditation Helps Soldiers and Their Family Members Find Serenity, December, 22, 2011, http://www.army.mil/article/71231/Living_in_the_here_and_now__mediation_helps_Soldiers__family_members_find_serenity/

Center for Contemplative Mind in Society. http://www.contemplativemind.org, 2012.

Chodron, Pema. *The Wisdom of No Escape*. Boston: Shambhala, 1991.

Chodron, Pema. *When Things Fall Apart*. Boston: Shambhala, 1991.

Chodron, Pema. *Start Where You Are: A Guide to Compassionate Living*. Boston: Shambhala, 1994.

Chodron, Pema. *The Places that Scare You: A Guide to Fearlessness in Difficult Times*. Boston: Shambhala, 2001.

Chodron, Pema. *Comfortable With Uncertainty*. Boston: Shambhala, 2002.

Cohen, Darlene. *Turning Suffering Inside Out: A Zen Approach to Living with Physical and Emotional Pain*. Boston: Shambhala, 2000.

Cohen, Darlene. *The One Who is not Busy: Connecting with Work in a Deep and Satisfying Way*. Salt Lake City, UT: Gibbs Smith, 2004.

Csikszentmilhalyi, Mihaly. *Flow: The Psychology of Optimal Experience*. New York: Harper and Row, 1990.

Csikszentmilhalyi, Mihaly. *Finding Flow: The Psychology of Engagement with Everyday Life*. New York: Basic, 1997.

Cullen, Lisa. "How to get Smarter, one Breath at a Time." *Time Magazine,* January 10, 2006, http://psyphz.psych.wisc.edu/web/News/Time_Jan06.html.

Das, Surya. *Buddha Standard Time: Awakening to the Infinite Possibilities.* New York: HarperOne, 2011.

Davidson, Richard, and others. "Alterations to Brain and Immune Functions Produced by Mindfulness Meditation." *Psychosomatic Medicine* 65, (2003): 564-570.

Davidson, Richard, and Jon Kabat-Zinn. "Response." *Psychosomatic Medicine* 66, (2004).

Der Hovanesian, Mara. "Zen and the Art of Corporate Productivity." *Business Week,* (July 28, 2003).

Deshimura, Taisen. *The Zen way to the Martial Arts.* (N. Amphoux, Trans.). New York: E.P. Dutton, 1982.

Dhamma Brothers. *Freedom Behind Bars,* 2007

Endler, Norman. "Person-situation Interaction and Anxiety." In *Handbook on Anxiety and Stress.* I. Dutach and L. Schlesinger, Washington: Jossey-Bass, 1980.

Epstein, Mark. *Thoughts Without A Thinker.* New York: Basic, 1995.

Fellman, Gordon. *Rambo and the Dalai Lama: The Compulsion to Win and Its Threat to Human Survival.* Albany: State University of New York Press, Albany, 1998.

Fenner, Perter. *The Edge of Certainty: Dilemmas on the Buddhist Path.* York Beach, ME: Nicholas-Hays, 2002.

Fields, Rick, Peggy Taylor, Rex Weyler, and Rick Ingrasce. *Chop Wood, Carry Water: A Guide to Finding Spiritual Fulfillment in Everyday Life.* New York: Tarcher, 1984.

Forbes, David. *Boyz to Buddhas.* New York: Peter Lang, 2004.

Fromm, Erich, D.T. Suzuki, and Richard De Martino. *Zen Buddhism and Psychoanalysis.* New York: Harper and Row, 1960.

Gibbs, J. J. *Dancing With Your Books: The Zen Way of Studying*. New York: Plume, 1990.

Gibbs, John. "Making Peace with Books." *Peace Review* 8, (1996): 577-580.

Golas, Thaddeus. *The Lazy Man's Guide to Enlightenment*. New York: Bantam, 1972.

Goldberg, Natalie. *Long Quiet Highway: Waking Up in America*. New York: Bantam, 1993.

Goldstein, Joseph. *The Experience of Insight Meditation*. Boston: Shambhala, 1987.

Goldstein, Joseph and Jack Kornfield. *Seeking the Heart of Wisdom: The Path of Insight Meditation*. Boston: Shambhala, 2001.

Goldstein, Joseph. *One Dharma*. New York: HarpersCollins, 2002.

Goleman, Daniel. *Emotional Intelligence*. New York: Bantam Books, 1995.

Graham, N. "Yoga for Credit." *The National Jurist* 15, (2006): 17-18.

Grossman, Paul, Ludger Niemann, Stefan Schmidt, and Harald Walach. "Mindfulness-based Stress Reduction and Health Benefits: A Meta-analysis." *Journal of Psychosomatic Research* 57, (2004): 35-43.

H. H. the Dalai Lama. *The Dalai Lama's Book of Wisdom*. New York: Thorsons, 2000.

Hamilton, Elizabeth. *Untrain Your Parrot*. Boston, MA: Shambhala, 2007.

Hanh, Thich Naht. *Being Peace*. Berkeley, CA: Parallax Press, 1987.

Hanh, Thich Naht. *Old Path White Clouds: Walking in the Footsteps of the Buddha*. Berkeley, CA: Parallax Press, 1991.

Hanh, Thich Naht. *Peace in Every Step*. New York: Bantam, 1991.

Hanh, Thich Naht. *Touching Peace: Practicing the Art of Mindful Living*. Berkeley, CA: Parallax Press, 1992.

Hanson, Rick with Rick Mendius. *Buddha's Brain*. Oakland, CA: New Harbinger, 2009.

Humphreys, Christmas. *Zen: A Way of Life*. Boston: Little Brown, 1962.

Humphreys, Christmas. *A Western Approach to Zen*. Wheaton, IL , 1971.

Humphreys, Christmas. *A Western Approach to Zen*. Wheaton, IL , 1974.

Jackson, Phil, and Hugh Delehanty. *Sacred Hoops: Spiritual Lessons of a Hardwood Warrior*. New York: Hyperion, 1996.

James, William. *Principles of Psychology*. New York: Holt, 1890.

Jobs, Steve. "Steve Jobs' 2005 Stanford Commencement Address." *Standford Report*, (June 14, 2005).

Johnson, Rodger, T. Johnson, and Karl Smith. *Cooperative Learning: Increasing College Facutly Instructional Productivity*. Self-published, 1991.

Johnston, James. "Look Inward, Attorney." *Legal Times* XXIX, no. 22 (May 29, 2006).

Jones, Ken. *Beyond Optimism: A Buddhist Political Ecology*. Oxford, UK: Jon Carpenter, 1993.

Jones, Ken. *The New Social Face of Buddhism: A Call to Action*. Somerville, MA: Wisdom, 2003.

Kabat-Zinn, Jon. *Full Catastrophe Living*. New York: Delta, 1990.

Kabat-Zinn, Jon. *Wherever You Go There You Are: Mindfulness Meditation in Everyday Life*. New York: Hyperion, 1994.

Kabat-Zinn, Jon. *Coming to our Senses: Healing Ourselves and the World through Mindfulness*. New York: Hyperion, 2005.

Kabat-Zinn, Jon. "Foreword" in McCown, Donald, Diane Reibel, and Marc Micozzi. *Teaching Mindfulness: A Practical Guide for Clinicians and Educators*. New York: Springer, 2011. xx-xxii.

Kabat-Zinn, Jon. *Mindfulness for Beginners*. Boulder, CO: Sounds True, 2012.

Kapleau, Roshi P. *The Three Pillars of Zen*. Garden City, NY: Anchor, 1980.

Kasulis, T. P. *Zen Action Zen Person*. Honolulu: The University Press of Hawaii, 1981.

Katagiri, Dainin. *Returning to Silence: Zen Practice in Daily Life*. Boston: Shambhala, 1988.

Katagiri, Dainin. *You Have Something to Say: Manifesting Zen Insight*. Boston: Shambhala, 1998.

Keeva, Steven. *Transforming Practices: Finding Joy and Satisfying in the Legal Life*. Chicago, IL: Contemporary Books, 1999.

Keightely, Alan. *Into Every Life a Little Zen Must Fall: A Christian Philosopher Looks to Alan Watts and the East*. London, UK: Wisdom, 1986.

Kennedy, Robert. *Zen Spirit, Christian Spirit: The Place of Zen in Christian Life*. New York: Bloomsbury Academic, 1995.

Khema, Ayya. *Be An Island: The Buddhist Practice of Inner Peace*. Somerville, MA: Wisdom, 1999.

Khema, Ayya. *Being Nobody, Going Nowhere.* Boston: Wisdom, 1987.

Knaus William. "Overcoming Procrastination" *University at Buffalo, Counseling Services,* 2005, http://ub-counseling.buffalo.edu/stressprocrast.shtml.

Kohn, Alfie. *Punished by Rewards: The Trouble with Gold Stars, Incentive Plans, A's, Praise and other Bribes.* New York: Houghton Mifflin Company, 1993.

Kornfield, Jack. *A Path With A Heart.* New York: Batam, 1993.

Kornfield, Jack. *After the Ecstasy, the Laundry: How the Heart Grows Wise on the Spiritual Path.* New York: Bantam, 2001.

Kozak, Arnie. *Wild Chickens and Petty Tyrants.* Somerville, MA: Wisdom, 2009.

Kraft, Kenneth. *Inner Peace, World Peace: Essays on Buddhism and Nonviolence.* Albany, NY: State University of New York Press, Albany, 1992.

Kumar, Sameet. *Grieving Mindfully: A Compassionate and Spiritual Guide to Coping with Loss.* Oakland, CA: Harbinger Publications, 2005.

Langer, Ellen. *Mindfulness.* Cambridge, MA: Perseus, 1989.

Langer, Ellen. *The Power of Mindful Learning.* Reading, MA: Addison-Wesley, 1997.

Lassalle, H. M. (Translated by John C. Maraldo). *Zen Meditation for Christians.* LaSalle, IL: Open Court Press, 1974.

Lazar, Sara, and others. "Meditation Experience is Associated with Increased Cortical Thickness." *NeuroReport* 16, 17 (2005): 1893-1897.

LeShan, Lawrence. *How to Meditate*. New York: Bantam Books, 1974.

Levine, Stephen. *A Year to Live*. New York: Bell Tower, 1977.

Linehan, Marsha, Hubert Armstrong, Alejandra Suarez, and Heidi Heard. "Cognitive- behavioral Treatment of Chronically Parasuicidal Borderline Patients." *Archives of General Psychiatry* 48, (1991): 1060-1064.

Lissen, Robert. *Zen: The Art of Life*. New York: Pyramid Communications, 1969.

Lohr, Steve. "A Techie, Absolutely, and More." *New York Times*, (2005), http://www.nytimes.com/2005/08/23/technology/23geeks.html.

Loori, John Daido. *Mountain Record of Zen Talks*. Boston: Shambhala, 1988.

Low, Albert. *Zen and Creative Management*. Garden City, NY: Anchor, 1976.

Loy, David. *The Great Awakening: A Buddhist Social Theory*. Somerville, MA: Wisdom, 2003.

Lozoff, Bo. *We're All Doing Time*. Durham, NC: Hanuman Foundation, 1985.

Lozoff, Bo, and Michael Braswell. *Inner Corrections: Finding Peace and Peace Making*. Cincinnati, OH: Anderson, 1989.

Macy, Joanna. *Mutual Causality in Buddhism and General Systems Theory: The Dharma of Natural Systems*. Albany, NY: State University of New York Press, Albany, 1991.

Macy, Joanna. *World as Lover, World as Self*. Berkeley, CA: Parallax Press, 1991.

Macy, Joanna and Molly Young Brown. *Coming Back to Life: Practices to Reconnect Our Lives, Our World*. Stony Creek, CA: New Society Publishers, 1998.

Maezumi, Taizan Hakuyu and Bernie Glassman. *The Hazy Moon of Enlightenment*. Somerville, MA: Wisdom, 2007.

Masunage, Rhiho. *A Primer of Soto Zen: A Translation of Dogen's Shobognezo Zuimonki*. Honolulu: The University of Hawaii Press, 1971.

Matthiessen, Peter. *Nine-Headed Dragon River*. Boston: Shambhala. 1985.

McCown, Donald, Diane Reibel, and Marc Micozzi. *Teaching Mindfulness: A Practical Guide for Clinicians and Educators*. New York: Springer, 2011.

McLeod, Ken. *Wake Up To Your Life*. New York: Haper-Collins, 2001.

McLeod, Melvin and the Editors of the Shambhala Sun, eds. *The Best Buddhist Writing 2004*. Boston: Shambhala, 2004.

McLeod, Melvin and the Editors of the Shambhala Sun, eds. *The Best Buddhist Writing 2011*. Boston: Shambhala, 2011.

McQuaid, John, and Paula Carmona. *Peaceful Mind: Using Mindfulness and Cognitive Behavioral Psychology to Overcome Depression*. Oakland, CA: New Harbinger, 2004.

Meditation Geek, "US Army intends to train 1.1 million US soldiers with meditation." March 18, 2010, http//www.meditationgeek.org/2010/03/us-army-intends-to-train-11-million-us.html.

Merriam-Webster. *Merriam-Webster's Collegiate Dictionary (10th ed.)*. Springfield, MA: Merriam-Webster, 1998.

Merton, Thomas. *Zen and the Birds of Appetite*. New York: New Directions Books, 1968.

Metcalf, Franz. *What Would Buddha Do?: 101 Answers to Life's Daily Dilemmas*. Berkeley, CA: Ulysses Press, 2002.

Metcalf, Franz. *Buddha in Your Backpack: Everyday Buddhism for Teens*. Berkeley, CA: Seastone, 2003.

Murphy, Bernadette. *Zen and the Art of Knitting*. Avon, MA: Adams Media, 2002.

Napoli, Lisa. "Buddhist Meditation: A Management Skill." *National Public Radio*, September 13, 2012, http://www.npr.org/2012/09/13/161050141/buddhist-meditation-a-management-skill.

Nussbaun, Martha. *Cultivating Humanity: A Classical Defense of Reform in Liberal Education*. Boston, MA: Harvard, 1997.

Packer, Toni. *The Work of this Moment*. Boston, MA: Shambhala, 1990.

Packer, Toni. *The Light of Discovery*. Boston, MA: Tuttle, 1995.

Packer, Toni. *The Silent Question*. Boston, MA: Shambhala, 2007.

Park, Chan. *Tango Zen: Walking Dance Meditation*. Sioux Falls, SD: Curled Up With a Good Book, 2005.

Park, Sung Bae. *Buddhist Faith and Sudden Enlightenment*. Albany, NY: State University of New York Press, Albany, 1983.

Parker-Pope, Tara. "Go Easy on Yourself, A New Wave of Research Urges." *New York Times*, February 28, 2011, http://well.blogs.nytimes.com/2011/02/28/go-easy-on-yourself-a-new-wave-of-research-urges/

Pirsig, Robert. *Zen and the Art of Motorcycle Maintenance*. New York: Bantam, 1974.

Prison Mindfulness Institute, Newsletter, Providence, RI, October, 2010.

Reasinger, Renee, and Sheila Brownlow. "Putting Off Until Tomorrow What is Better Done Today: Academic Procrastination as a Function of Motivation toward College Work." Poster Presented at the Annual Meeting of the Southwestern Psychological Association, Norfolk, VA, March, 1996.

Reynolds, David. *Playing Ball on Running Water: Living Morita Psychotherapy.* New York: Quill, 1984.

Riskin, Leonard. "The Contemplative Lawyer: On the Potential Contributions of Mindfulness Meditation to Law Students, Lawyers and their Clients." *Harvard Negotiation Law Review* 7, no. 1 (2002): 1-66.

Rohe', Fred. *The Zen of Running.* New York: Random House, 1974.

Rosenaum, Elana. *Being Well: Mindfulness Practices for People with Cancer and Other Serious Illnesses.* Boston: Shambhala, 2012.

Rosenberg, Larry, and David Guy. *Breath by Breath: The Liberation Practice of Insight Meditation.* Boston, MA: Shambhala, 1998.

Rosenberg, Larry, and David Guy. *Living in the Light of Death: The Art of Being Truly Alive.* Boston: Shambhala, 2000.

Ryan, Richard M., Kennon M. Sheldon, Tim Kasser, and Edward L. Deci. "All Goals were not Created Equal: An Organismic Perspective on the Nature of Goals and their Regulation." In *Psychology of Action: Linking Motivation and Cognition to Behavior,* edited by Peter. M. Gollwitzer and John. A. Bargh, 7-26. New York: Guildford, 1995.

Ryan, Tim. *Mindful Nation*. Carlsbad, CA: Hay House, 2012.

Salzberg, Sharon. *A Heart as Wide as the World: Living with Mindfulness, Wisdom, and Compassion*. Boston: Shambahla, 1997.

Salzberg, Sharon. *Voices of Insight: Teachers of Buddhism in The West Share Their Wisdom, Stories, and Experiences of Insight Meditation*. Boston: Shambahla, 1999.

Salzberg, Sharon. *Lovingkindness: The Revolutionary Art of Happiness* Boston: Shambahla, 2002.

Schon, Donald A. *Displacement of Concepts*. London: Tavistock, 1963.

Schumacher, E. F. *A Guide For The Perplexed*. New York: Harper & Row, 1977.

Schumacher, E. F. *Small Is Beautiful: Economics as if People Mattered*. New York: Harper Perennial, 1989.

Shaku, Soyen. *Zen for Americans*. Peru, IL: Open Court Publishing, 1906.

Shapiro, Shauna, Kirk Warren Brown, and John A. Astin. *Toward the Integration of Meditation into Higher Education*. Center for Contemplative Mind in Society, 2008.

Shoshanna, Brenda. *Zen and the Art of Falling in Love*. New York: Simon & Schuster, 2003.

Simmer-Brown, Judith, and Fran Grace. *Meditation and the Classroom: Contemplative Pedagogy for Religious Studies*. Albany, NY: State University of New York Press, Albany.

Sutton, Robert. *Weird Ideas that Work: 11 1/2 Practices for Promoting, Management, and Sustaining Innovation*. New York: Free Press, 2002.

Suzuki, Shunryu. *Zen Mind, Beginner's Mind.* New York, NY: Weatherhill, 1970.

The University of Chicago News Office, "Writing About Worries Eases Anxiety and Improves Test Performance." January 13, 2011.

Tollifson, Joan. *Bare-Bones Meditation.* New York: Bell Tower, 1996.

Trout, Kilgore. *Venus on the Half Shell.* New York: Bantam Dell, 1974.

Trungpa, Chogyam. *Shambhala: The Sacred Path of the Warrior.* Boston: Shambhala, 1984.

University of Illinois at Urbana-Champaign. "Self-help Brochures: Procrastination." Counseling Center, 2002, http://www.couns.uiuc.edu/brochures/procras.htm.

University of Massachusetts Medical School. Center for Mindfulness in Medicine, Health Care, and Society (CFM), 2006, http://umassmed.edu.

Wallace, Allan B. *The Attention Revolution: Unlocking the Power of the Focused Mind.* Somerville, MA: Wisdom, 2006.

Watts, Alan. *The Wisdom of Insecurity: A Message for the Age of Anxiety.* New York: Vintage, 1951.

Whitney, Kobai Scott. *Sitting Inside: Buddhist Practice in America's Prisons.* Boulder, CO: Prison Dharma Network, 2002.

Wilber, Ken. *Sex, Ecology, Spirituality: The Spirit of Evolution.* Boston: Shambhala, 1995.

Wilber, Ken. *The Eye of the Spirit: An Integral Vision for a World Gone Slightly Mad.* Boston: Shambhala, 1997.

Wilber, Ken. *A Theory of Everything: An Integral Vision for Business, Politics, Science and Spirituality.* Boston: Shambhala, 2000.

Wilber, Ken. *Boomeritis.* Boston: Shambhala, 2002.

Wilber, Ken. *Kosmic Consciouness.* (Speaker Interviewed, 10 CD Set: #AF00758D). Boulder, CO: Sounds True, 2003.

Wilson, Jeff. "The Wilderness of the Mind." *Tricycle: The Buddhist Review* XIV, no. 1 (2004), 24-25.

Wilson, Timothy D., and Daniel T. Gilbert. "Affective Forecasting: Knowing What to Want." *Current Directions in Psychological Science* 14, no. 3 (2005): 131-134.

Winston, Diana. *Wide Awake: A Buddhist Guide for Teens.* New York: Perigee, 2003.

Wisdom 2.0. "The Rise and Benefits of Mindfulness." *Wisdom 2.0,* June 23, 2009, http://wisdom2.net/2009/06/the-rise-and-benefits-of-mindfulness/

Zarefsky, David. *Argumentation: the Study of Effective Reasoning.* Chantilly, VA: The Teaching Company, 2005.

CPSIA information can be obtained
at www.ICGtesting.com
Printed in the USA
LVHW051434070219
606760LV00016B/520/P

9 780989 531412